CW00323833

Child Protection in Early Childhood Services

Papers from two seminars organised by
The Early Childhood Unit and
The Child Abuse Training Unit in
London and Leeds
March 1993

**Edited by Gillian Pugh
and Anne Hollows**

The National Children's Bureau was established as a registered charity in 1963. Our purpose is to identify and promote the interests of all children and young people and to improve their status in a diverse society.

We work closely with professionals and policy makers to improve the lives of all children but especially young children, those affected by family instability, children with special needs or disabilities and those suffering the effects of poverty and deprivation.

We collect and disseminate information about children and promote good practice in children's services through research, policy and practice development, publications, seminars, training and an extensive library and information service.

The Bureau works in partnership with Children in Wales and Children in Scotland.

ISBN 1 874579 19 9

Published by the National Children's Bureau, 8 Wakley Street, London EC1V 7QE. Telephone 071 278 9441. Registered charity number 258825.

Typeset by Books Unlimited – Rainworth, Notts, NG21 0JE.

Printed by Saxon Graphics Ltd, Derby, DE21 4SZ

Contents

List of figures

Introduction

Anne Hollows, Child Abuse Training Unit,
Gillian Pugh, Early Childhood Unit
National Children's Bureau

The term 'early childhood services' encompasses a rich and diverse range of provision. It includes childminders, playgroups, day nurseries, family centres and nursery schools and classes, services that are run within the statutory sector through local authority education and social services departments, through the health sector and in the voluntary and private sectors. The wide ranging activities which cluster within the term 'early childhood services' make it a logical and obvious location for expertise and activity in child protection work. Here we have services for the youngest and most vulnerable members of the population: those least able to protect themselves or to tell of their experiences. Here, too, we have professionals with an extraordinary range of practice skills and experience in the care of very young children as well as in working closely with parents and carers of children. And yet the very fact that so many cases of abuse and death of children under eight years of age continue to take place, suggests that staff in early years services may not know how to recognise abuse, may not understand what children are trying to tell them and may not know what to do about it. It also suggests that while their professional commitment is to ensuring that children can maximise their development and be safe, the links between this and the prevention of child abuse are not always apparent.

Early childhood services operate at the sharp end of intervention with parents and children. Many nurseries and pre-school groups incorporate creative and sensitive strategies to work with young children and their families which should be much better understood and recognised by child protection specialists. The contact time that nursery workers have with children and their parents is vastly in excess of anything offered by a social worker, doctor or health visitor. They see the child in all her or his moods: in happiness, frustration, excitement, anger and in fear. They will observe and note changes over time so that these can be set against external standards and information about adults in the child's life. Most critically they work in environments which are full of children and can form a view about an individual child which is grounded in their knowledge of the wider group of children and overall patterns of child development.

Early childhood services are often used by professionals in health and social services as part – often the major part – of protection plans for young children. While these services will have highly specialised staff who can deploy a wide range of sensitive skills in their work with children and families, they may have little knowledge about key issues in protecting children. Because the nature of the role and their skills is so often misunderstood by the professionals who bear the statutory responsibility for protecting children, early years workers sometimes report feelings of being excluded from the serious activities of planning and deciding about the future for children and families when abuse is suspected. Out on a limb, as some of those who work in early childhood services find themselves to be, they cannot integrate their work with that of the other professionals involved in a family. If their professional judgement is not valued and used, then child protection services will lose access to vital information about risks and strengths in the families who are causing concern as well as risking alienating the support and potential involvement of those who work on a regular day to day basis with children.

There are other problem areas too. Recent months have seen evidence that occasionally the adults who work in early years settings may themselves pose dangers to children. Experience in other sectors of care has shown that it is difficult to ensure recruitment strategies which will guarantee against such people being employed. We have no doubt that blanket exclusions of, for example, male workers or students would ultimately limit the quality of the experience offered to children. The knowledge that these events do, however rarely, take place is fundamental to the power to prevent them and points to the need for Area Child Protection Committees to place a high priority on ensuring that these services are safe for the children – sometimes particularly vulnerable children – that they serve. This means ensuring that staff are all aware of the potential threat to children's safety and well being and that responsibility for safe practice is embraced throughout the organisations which sponsor and maintain early childhood services.

In some ways the work of the Child Abuse Training Unit and the Early Childhood Unit at the National Children's Bureau has mirrored issues identified here. Busily working on our own remits we have had little time to pause and look at how our interests might beneficially converge. But we did, in the spring of 1993, make the time to organise two seminars where keynote speakers and workshop sessions explored the issues in depth. Now we have brought together papers from the speakers and workshops in the aim of reaching a wider audience than the two seminars. We believe that the papers contain valuable information as well as setting the agenda for future work in this area.

In our desire to ensure universal access to services for children in their early years we must recognise that these services can offer protection for children, as well as promoting and nurturing their development. The long term prevention of child abuse and neglect will depend in some measure upon this. Our task in publishing these papers is to promote the potential of early childhood services and the key role of those who work within them in this vital work with young children and their families.

Keynote presentations

1. Key issues in diagnosis and response in child abuse

Dr Chris Hobbs, Consultant Paediatrician
St James' Hospital Leeds

If prevention of child abuse is to be a reality, then work with families with pre-school children must be given a high priority. This paper will look at the process of diagnosis of child abuse and how recognition can be turned into effective intervention.

Diagnosis used in a medical sense denotes the process or pathology and is a necessary prerequisite for medical treatment.

Symptoms described by the patient and signs observed by the doctor combine with investigations (for example, laboratory, x-ray) to provide an answer to the question 'what is the matter'.

Once a diagnosis is established, then treatment and also prognosis (future outlook) follow.

Diagnosis

Diagnosis in child abuse shares similarities to the medical model and involves:

- recognising the harmful effects of damaging interactions of a physical, sexual or psychological kind;
- assessing the severity and significance of harm suffered;
- exploring ways in which the child can be protected;
- thinking about other children who may be at risk.

Management and treatment are issues which usually follow diagnosis.

It is important to remember that the central issues in child protection work are:

- the harm the child suffers;
- the protection of the child;

(that is, the welfare of the child is paramount).

Who has harmed the child and what is to be done with him or her is of importance with regard to other children and to the criminal justice system but should not be allowed to obscure these other considerations.

The harmful effects of child abuse can be observed in:

- physical injuries, for example, bruises, fractures, brain injury;
- sexual injuries, sexually transmitted infections;
- psychological harm manifested in a disturbance of the child's intellectual and emotional development;
- changes in the child's behaviour;
- failure of the child to grow and develop to his or her full potential;
- distortion of the normal patterns of social development, for example, attachment, abusive or antisocial behaviour to others;
- a tendency to repeat the cycle of abuse in the next generation.

It is because of the wide ranging effects of child abuse on the developing child that it is always important to approach the issue of diagnosis from various aspects. For this reason the preferred approach involves the gradual building of a jigsaw picture and Fig 1.1 provides an outline of the investigatory pathway.

The jigsaw model (Fig 1.2)

The jigsaw model provides a method by which all information and understanding about a child can be assembled in a way that enables abuse to be recognised and at the same time reveals the next important issues to be addressed in order for the child to be protected.

As the jigsaw is assembled a picture is revealed. It may at first be a confusing and difficult picture to make sense of, and pieces may be missing. However it is important that professionals do share information with one another openly and be willing to report concerns which includes speaking out at case conferences.

Figure 1.1   Investigating a case of possible child abuse – an outline

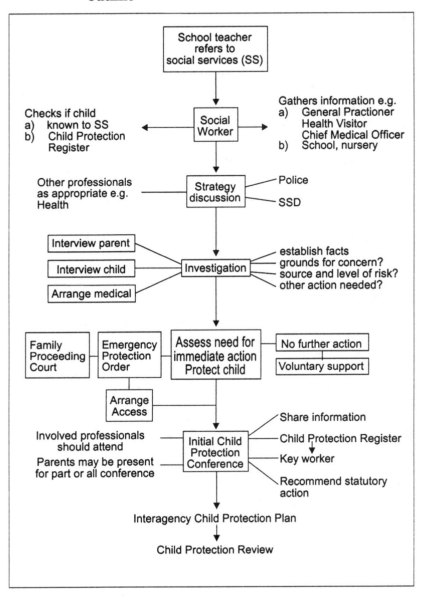

Figure 1.2   The jigsaw of sexual abuse

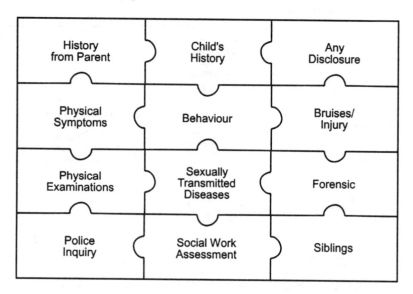

Case history

An infant of two months was presented at hospital with a painful arm which he would not use. An x-ray reveals a small hairline fracture of the humerus bone. The parents explain that the child slipped while they were bathing him the previous evening. The baby appeared to be all right but the following morning cried when being dressed.

The parents seemed concerned and respectable. The mother did all the talking. The doctor in the hospital knew about child abuse and was a little concerned because of the infant's age. However because the history seemed reasonable he did nothing else.

The next day a more senior doctor noted that, in addition to the arm fracture, also visible on the x-ray were two healing rib fractures of an older age than the arm injury. The parents were contacted and further investigations were pursued.

Here one piece of jigsaw was not felt to be enough, but two pieces changed the whole management of the case and other pieces were then sought. Additional information soon followed including poor growth which was an important piece already held by the health visitor.

Case conferences should assist in assembling the picture. Are professionals as able to share all their information now that parents are present? I suspect that they are not in many cases. Do professionals now spend more time in case conferences but say less? The answer to one of these questions is that more time is taken with parents present (20 minutes according to research yet to be published by Margaret Bell of York University). The other questions are harder to answer.

Child abuse diagnosis can be difficult because families and professionals protect themselves against the difficult feelings which abuse engender.

Psychological mechanisms include 'denial' – it did not happen, there is nothing the matter with this child/family/parents; and 'dissociation' – I can't feel a thing, it isn't real, this leg isn't hurting (really there is a fracture).

These mechanisms are not only encountered in children and parents but also in professionals sharing these stresses. Professionals may inadvertently collude because it is difficult to keep listening and receiving the anger. Reassuring and keeping people happy has no place in helping with these difficult problems. Recently a mother told me I had seen bruises in a child which did not exist. She had taken the child to the GP who agreed that there were no bruises although the child was seen the same day and the bruises were recent when I saw them. She even told me that she had no doubt about my competence. The GP wrote to social services to say there were no bruises. Why was it so important for the mother and the GP to pretend there were no bruises?

Switching off (disconnecting one's awareness from the thought, act, feeling) is important as a mechanism for defence. Some children at medical examinations may completely switch off and appear to go to sleep. What does this tell about earlier experiences?

Summit (1983) described the accommodation syndrome which helps to explain some of the psychological accompaniments of abuse. Our experience is that the most severely abused children are often the least obviously distressed on the surface. They are compliant and passive.

It is being acknowledged that these children can carry on outwardly their lives as though nothing was happening to them but it makes their credibility ratings very low according to our common sense when they try and tell us what has been happening to them. The doctor may see unusual medical symptoms with no obvious physical cause (for example, 'I can see double', 'I can't use this leg') and worrying anal signs indicating injury but the school and neighbours see this cheerful chatty child who is top of her class. At the case meeting the different sides of the child will be reflected in the professional dichotomy of view. We are very worried on the one hand, we are very happy with little Lucy on the other. How does the child keep these two parts of herself separately functioning and at what price?

Important jigsaw pieces in abuse

Physical abuse is observed predominantly in younger children, with infants having the highest levels of serious injury and death. Any physical injury in a baby must always be looked at carefully. Some fractures for example, rib, femur, skull, humerus seem so linked with abuse that skilful assessment seems mandatory in virtually every case.

Case history

A baby with brochiolitis had a chest x-ray during a hospital admission for treatment of this infection. This revealed two old and healing rib fractures. Such fractures usually only occur as a result of injury and not as part of the illness. No history of injury makes abuse very likely. Because the infant had not been presented because of concerns regarding abuse it was more difficult for the doctor to discuss his concerns with the parents. The result was that the child was sent home without a case conference.

Much abuse is hidden so the opportunity must be taken when it avails itself to intervene. Much harm can ensue before another opportunity presents itself.

Normal development and children's usual experience must be understood if injury is to be assessed. Thirty to 40 per cent of 'normal children' examined in surveys have some kind of injury including one or two bruises or a scratch or laceration and one per cent have a recent burn. Bruises to the face (toddlers' forehead bruises an exception) are uncommon and injury less common after three years.

Bruises in abuse

Bruises are present in 90 per cent of physically abused children. They are more difficult to detect in dark skins, and naturally go through a process of change in colour from red/blue to purple to green brown/yellow as they age. There is no set time limit but for up to 48 hours bruises tend to be swollen and blue/red. They may last for as long as two to three weeks although usually disappear well before this. In abuse there may be a larger than usual number, they may be of different or the same age if a single assault, and be found in sites not usually associated with injury. The explanation of how they have been caused may not fit – with size, shape, age and so on. Inflicted bruises may be:

- hand marks (punch, slap, grip, pinch, poke) and each has a different appearance;
- mark of an implement – shoe, strap, buckle, flex or stick;
- bruises from pushing, throwing, or swinging child against a hard object;
- bite marks – semicircular often paired marks which may show individual tooth impressions if fresh;
- kicks – larger bruises, rounded often on legs or trunk;
- bizarre marks unlike anything commonly seen following an accident. The commonest includes petechial or pin-prick bruises which arise from unusual pressure rupturing small blood vessels in the skin.

Important sites

In abuse the face and head are most often injured. Bruises to the cheeks, ear lobes and surrounding skin, lower jaw, around the eyes, mouth, including lips and teeth, neck and scalp are all common. The forehead can be bruised, for example when the child is pushed against a wall and blood can track down around both eyes (two black eyes). Strangulation marks can be seen around the neck as well as 'love bites' in sexual abuse.

Bruises to the chest wall and abdomen are unusual accidentally but linked strongly to abuse where the child is gripped or nipped. Lower abdominal bruises are strongly linked to sexual abuse.

The upper and lower parts of the arms and legs may be gripped or hit whereas below the elbow and knee an accidental knock may leave a bruise, particularly if it is against the bone which lies superficially under the skin of the forearm and shin. Finally the soft and padded buttocks are not so often bruised accidentally but this is another common site in abuse. Bruises to the abdomen, genital area and outside and inside the thigh are linked with sexual abuse when the child is gripped and held.

Burns and scalds, for example, from spilt cups of tea in toddlers are all too common but other burns such as grid mark contact burn on the back of hand may need the limb to be held against the hot object. Sometimes children are immersed into hot water leaving glove or stocking scalds to the limbs or scalds to the bottom with a spared central area (like a hole in a doughnut) where the skin has been pressed against the cold bath bottom.

Sexual abuse (CSA)

Sexual abuse is another important and common aspect of child abuse with many adults giving a retrospective history of childhood abuse. Both boys and girls are abused, the peak age being two to six years. Abusers are usually known well to the child, being family members in two third of cases, teenagers in a quarter. Increasingly women are also being recognised as abusers.

The jigsaw (see Fig 1.2) includes:

- a history from the parents;
- statement or disclosure by the child;
- physical symptoms;
- changes in behaviour;
- sexually transmitted disease;
- physical injury, physical examination findings (genital and anal);
- forensic tests;
- social work assessment;
- police inquiry; and
- an examination and assessment of siblings or other children in contact.

Children disclose sexual abuse as and when they decide to and this is often delayed and frequently retracted. Informal comments to chosen confidants when the child is relaxed and feels safe are not always repeated to unknown (albeit skilled, caring and professional) interviewers working in formal settings.

There are many ways that children communicate their experience of sexual abuse:

- make an ambiguous statement for example, 'a little girl I know';
- sexually explicit play in a pre-school child;
- drop hints for example 'I want to tie my daddy's hands';
- in older child, sexually precocious behaviour and prostitution;
- become ill – develop a psychosomatic disorder;
- undergo a change in behaviour;
- start to wet or soil;
- make a direct statement (disclosure);
- put themself in danger, self injure, overdose, run away;
- become an abuser, for example while babysitting;
- as an adult develop psychiatric disorder, abuse alcohol, drugs, prostitution, psychosexual disorder, suicide.

Disclosures may be precipitated at any time and occur in a variety of circumstances:

- during a sex education talk or TV programme;
- because of changes in home circumstances – parents split up, move to foster care and so on;
- through casual comment in a young child 'did you know?';
- because of fear of escalating abuse, leading perhaps to pregnancy;
- through fear of returning home when the child is protected;
- as an attempt to protect other children, particularly siblings.

Young pre-school children's disclosures of sexual abuse are often more difficult to hear. The child may be confused about what is happening, or not have any real understanding of what is happening and lack the vocabulary to attempt an explanation. Their explanation may be limited to pointing at their genital area or bottom and indicating that it hurts, perhaps linking it to saying somebody (for example, daddy) hurt. A commonly heard explanation is 'he hurt my bottom with a knife'. This can confuse the listener because there is no cut or blood and it may be dismissed because it doesn't make immediate sense. Another better recognised example is where the child says that 'he weed on the bed'.

In other situations the child tries to explain the sexual act(ion). For example the repeated thrusting movement can be linked to another repetitive reciprocating action the child has witnessed for example, banging nails in with a hammer so 'he hurt me with a hammer'. Ask the child to demonstrate what was meant. The use of dolls (anatomically and non-anatomically complete) does provide the child with a means of demonstrating what they may be trying to say but the dolls, which have come in for criticism, should not be used by untrained persons.

Having drawing materials available allows some children another means of expression of images in their minds which otherwise could not be easily communicated. Many who work with sexually abused children comment on the number of drawings they see with phallus like images but most would not present such material in court.

Physical symptoms include:

- Anal: pain on defecation, bleeding, discharge, redness, soreness, constipation, stool withholding, waddling gait, pain on walking. The anus may appear sore and red, gaping, there may be distended veins incorrectly labelled "haemorrhoids". Prolapse may occur. (This can occur, like some of these other signs, in different conditions not linked to abuse).
- Genital (boys): soreness, bruising, splits in the foreskin, bleeding, redness.
- Genital (girls): soreness, pain on passing urine (usually there is no infection in the urine), complaints of specific pain in the genital area, bleeding (commonest cause in prepubertal child is CSA), 'early period' when child shows no signs of pubertal development, observation of gaping open appearance.
- Emotional and behavioural symptoms will vary according to age, and to some extent gender. A wide range of symptoms have been reported from non-specific ones such as wetting and abdominal pains to specific ones as detailed below for the pre-school child.

Specific emotional and behavioural indications of sexual victimisation

Pre-school (0-4 years)

- Nightmares triggered by place, person, objects related or including physical movements or vocalisations that are consistent with abusive experiences.
- Premature eroticisation:

  — preoccupation with genitals;
  — repetitive seeking to engage others in differentiated sexual behaviour;
  — excessive or indiscriminate masturbation with or without objects;
  — precocious apparently seductive behaviour;
  — depiction of differentiated sexual acts in doll play.

- Fearfulness:

  — over-determined denial of genital anatomy and exposure to normal nudity;
  — avoidance and anxiety in response to specific questions about differentiated sexual behaviour;
  — unexplained person, gender, place or object avoidance or fearfulness.

- Child's age appropriate and circumstantially congruent description of being sexually abused.
- Dissociative phenomena.

Less specific indicators include somatic complaints, abdominal pains, headaches, double vision, mysterious unexplained pains that are only relieved by a nocturnal visit by mother, sleep disorders, nightmares, crying out in the sleep, wetting – day or night, soiling, social withdrawal, hyperactivity, changes in school behaviour, poor concentration, over achievement and low attendance in school, aggressiveness, hostility, cruelty to other children or animals, running away, substance abuse, self-mutilation (can start in pre-school years), eating disorders (obesity, anorexia), delinquency, lying and others.

These symptoms often occurring over months or years are important in diagnosis. The medical examination has been at the centre of the controversy over the widespread nature of CSA. This area has recently been reviewed in reports of the American Academy of Paediatrics (1991) and the Royal College of Physicians (1991). It is common for there to be pressure for the doctor to say dogmatically whether the child has been abused and for a long time the medical examination was viewed as a means of corroborating a child's statement. Without medical evidence the investigation would have ground to a halt. Now it is not necessary for the child's evidence to be corroborated because the witness is a child but it may still have to be corroborated because of the nature of the offence itself. Pressure therefore still remains on the doctor to be too dogmatic. Often the medical examination only provides evidence which will add to the overall picture.

There is an increasing acceptance that children do tell the truth about CSA but children are still exposed to vigorous and hostile cross examination in the witness box so that for many children an appearance is just not possible. Although there are some exceptions, including some very young children, our experience in Leeds has been that successful prosecutions have fallen from 17 per cent in 1985/6 to 5 per cent in 1989 and remain low (see Appendix 1.1). This is clearly a cause for concern and one which all the recent changes in the law has had little positive effect upon. This demonstrates the high burden of proof and the need for child witnesses. The use of videotapes is unlikely to alter this situation as children are still needed for cross-examination.

Most of the work as a paediatrician in this area relates to protection offered through the family proceedings courts where all one's expertise can be brought to play. The paediatric task includes the full medical method of history and examination as expressed in the jigsaw. Appreciating the child's psychological functioning, behaviour, growth and development are as important and crucial as counting bruises and measuring the hymenal opening.

Of course children who are being sexually abused may present in many ways, including with symptoms to a doctor. Faced with a child with symptoms and signs suggestive of abuse the doctor faces some important decisions and judgements. When is the concern sufficient to refer to a statutory authority? If it is too soon and premature abortive investigation occurs, then the case may close up and be lost. Late referral leaves the child unprotected in the short term. I now have several children who I have been following with concerns but where referral was delayed until more work had been done around the child's problems.

There are some guidelines available (Fig 1.3). A joint clinic with a psychologist has helped with these difficult cases.

Figure 1.3 Guidelines for making the decision to report CSA (American Academy of Paediatrics 1991 and Royal College of Physicians 1991)

History	Examination	Laboratory findings	Concern	Report
none	normal	none	none	none
behavioural changes	normal	none	low	± FU
none	supportive	none	possible	± FU
history from parents	supportive	none	possible	± FU
none	diagnostic	none	probable	refer
clear statement	normal	none	probable	refer
clear statement	diagnostic	none	probable	refer
none	normal} supportive} diagnostic}	gonorrhoea} semen} pregnancy}	definite}	refer}
behavioural changes	supportive	other STD	probable	refer

Notes:
1. Supportive, for example enlarged hymenal opening.
2. Diagnostic, for example laceration of anus.
3. FU – follow up if continuing concerns.
4. If in doubt discuss with colleagues and senior social worker.
5. Refer = to social services (child also followed up).

Sexually transmitted diseases

For a long time it was thought that childhood infection with these diseases which are usually transmitted through sexual activity in adulthood, occurred by accident, for example through towels, toilet seats. However a careful study in 1965 by Branch and Paxton revealed a sexual contact in virtually every case of gonorrhoea studied in one to ten-year-old children.

The prevalence of STD in sexually abused children varies from study to study from one to two percent to 18 per cent. Other infections include herpes, syphilis, trichomonas, chlamydia, genital warts and AIDS, see Figure 1.4. One author showed that of 96 children tested positive for HIV virus, 14 acquired their infection by CSA. In another study 15 children were sexually abused by an HIV positive perpetrator and three converted to positive. When these infections are encountered, an investigation into CSA is needed.

The sexually abused battered child

An important association exists between CSA and non-accidental non-genital injury. Ten per cent of sexually abused children in a recent study presented with physical abuse. Hobbs and Wynne looked at 2883 children referred to paediatricians over a four-year period.

There were 769 physically abused, 949 sexually abused and 130 both physically and sexually abused children.

- one in six physically abused children were also sexually abused.
- one in seven sexually abused children were also physically abused.

The children were young, with the average age of the boys at 6.8 years, and girls at 5.7. Fewer older sexually abused children were injured but one 13-year-old girl and one four-year-old boy were murdered by their mother's partners.

The study revealed a pattern of injuries which differed from that seen in a group of physically abused children. 'Love bites', bruises around breasts, other bites, and bruising around abdomen, buttocks, thighs and knees as pinch or grip marks or scratches were found. Burns are also important and often denote a sadistic ele-

Figure 1.4 Sexually transmitted diseases and the probability of abuse

STD	Incubation period	Vertical transmission- neonatal disease	Probability of abuse (after RCP 1991)
Gonorrhoea	three to four days	neonatal ophthalmia neonatal vaginitis (rare)	XX (XXX if child less than two years)
Trichomonas	one to four weeks	rare but occasionally seen, usually clears spontaneously	XXX
Chlamydia	seven to 14 days	neonatal conjunctivitis neonatal pneumonitis	XX (XXX if child less than three years and organism cultured is child's)
Condyloma Acuminata (genital warts)	several months	laryngeal papillomata (HPV-II)	X
Herpes	two to 14 days	localised or disseminated	XX
Bacterial vaginosis	two to 14 days		X
HIV	majority convert in three months	if maternal	sexual assault
Hepatitis B	up to three months	infection	recognised
Syphilis	up to three months		XXX

Footnotes:
1. Key: X – possible, XX – likely CSA, XXX – almost certain CSA
2. The former presumed importance of fomites is decreasing.
3. Full penetrative sexual intercourse (vaginal or anal) is not necessary for infection. Orogenital sex and intercrural contact may transmit pathogens.

ment to the abuse – these children are tortured and terrified and need urgent protection.

Four children in all were murdered all within the home and anal findings were found in three.

Links to other maltreatment

It is important to recognise that the different kinds of child abuse overlap enormously. It is important to ask in what way is the child being neglected. Almost always the child who is sexually or physically ill-treated is also psychologically ill-treated as well. He is likely to be rejected, scapegoated, likened to his violent father or 'to have the devil in him'. (What does that mean to the child?) In sexual abuse the child is manipulated to feel responsible or guilty, and threats are made for the child to keep the secret. The child may be bribed and can be corrupted into accepting affection, favours and power in exchange for sexual use.

The emotionally abused child can be deprived of love, food or both. Failure to thrive (Fig 1.5) refers to the situation where the child fails to grow in the expected way and these children are deprived of food and experience emotionally harmful interactions with their parents.

Figure 1.5 Causes and effects of failure to thrive (from Hanks and Hobbs, 1993)

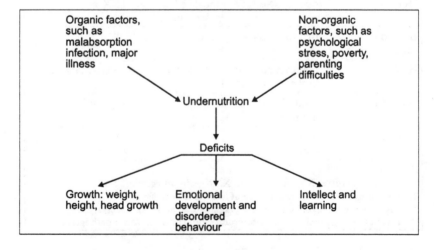

The consequences are impairment of the child's development, usually with weight at or below the third centile, short stature and poor head growth. The child may resemble a much younger child although will not necessarily look thin, wasted or malnourished in the way that is often expected. These children have in the past been referred to as deprivation dwarfs or psychosocially short stature children. There is often poor attachment to their mothers. They may show a range of behaviours. One of the commonest is that they are constantly on the go – as though perpetually searching. They are tiring to look after, sleep fitfully and wear out their carers. Some of these children were withdrawn and shirk contact with adults, whilst others indiscriminately express their strong and unmet needs by putting their arms out to anyone who passes. Catching up growth in a good foster home or sometimes in the hospital confirms the capacity to grow normally but requires supernormal calorie intake (1.5 to 2 x normal for weight and age).

Emotionally ill-treated children show patterns of symptoms or maladaptations which vary with age:

Child's age (years)	Guidelines to child's symptoms or maladaptations
0–1	sleep/feeding problems, irritability, apathy, dull, anxious attachment
1–3	as above; overactive, apathetic, aggressive, attention deficit, language delay, indiscriminate affection, fearful and anxious, inability to play, irritable, anxious and ambivalent attachments
3–6	as above, peer relationship difficulties, attention seeking, clingy, school failure begins, poor social skills
6–12	as above – sleep/feeding problems may resolve, inappropriate attachment to carers, rejected by peers, school failure, delinquent behaviour, running away, truanting, wetting, soiling, stealing, bullying
12+	as above, depressions escalated aggression, anxiety, overdosing, poor self image, weting, soiling, psychosomatic illness, drug and substance abuse, criminal acts.

Siblings: Do we need to assess?

It is common clinical experience that it is unusual for only one child in a family to be abused as most abuse is by a family member or someone in close contact with the child and his family.

Muram and Speck (1991) looked at a policy of examining all children closely associated with a victim or perpetrator of sexual abuse even if they (or a parent) denied involvement.

Abuse of siblings/associates

In the first six months all contacts were examined.

Results:
Primary victims   188 girls
Siblings   59 girls (average age, whole group
                    = 6.5 years)

Results (genital physical findings related to abuse):

	Specific %	Non-specific %	Normal %
Victims	42	27	31
Siblings	68	8	24

Of 59 associates, 50 were interviewed, 24 disclosed were also victims of abuse. There was no predictive value in genital abnormality and subsequent disclosure.

Special groups: Children with disabilities

Are there any children who are especially vulnerable to abuse? Valerie Sinason (1993) describes the way in which society speedily changes its terms for mental handicap (learning disability) because of the contamination of the meaning and nature of the words. This is largely because of the difficulty which society has in coping with the differences between normal and disabled. Many studies have shown that abuse is much more prevalent in this group than the general population. Kennedy (1990) quoted studies from the USA in which 54 per cent of boys and 50 per cent of girls in the deaf population reported abuse. Abuse can be itself a cause of disability

(VIMH – violence induced mental handicap – was a term used by Buchanan and Oliver (1979) because 3-11 per cent of a group of children they studied had mental handicap caused by abuse or neglect).

Increasing number of cases are now being reported of abuse of children and adults with disabilities and pressure should be brought to bear for greater justice and protection for these people under the legal system.

The current response to child abuse in the UK

The past decade has seen a substantial increase in the recognition of child abuse. A decade ago sexual abuse was virtually unreported, and there was far fewer children on the child protection registers. In 1985 the NSPCC reported that three children die at the hands of their parents each week or approximately 150 per year. Newspaper reports in 1991 continue to identify many (probably no fewer) children who died of non-accidental injury in England, Scotland and Wales. Greater recognition does not necessarily mean greater protection. There is evidence that under the new Children Act the number of child protection orders had fallen from 6,000 to about 1,600 and fewer children are the subject of legal proceedings. In Leeds which has one of the busiest care courts in the country, cases of infants with unexplained fractures have been allowed to remain at home without legal proceedings being initiated, reflecting the major changes in the child protection system which have been taking place in the past few years.

There are those who interpret the reduction in legal proceedings and more recently the fall in numbers of children on child protection registers to mean that the system is working better. The worry is that the reverse is the case – fewer children are being protected. The extra resources needed to keep children safely at home are not always available. Court cases are becoming more complex and lasting longer (the last case I was involved with took over six weeks to hear and whilst it is desirable that everyone has a fair say, it means that other work does not get done).

At the present time the most pressing need is for more therapeutic resources to treat children and their families. Again quoting our research in Leeds (Frothingham and others, 1993) only 25 per cent of all sexually abused children had any kind of therapeutic help outside that which their keyworker could offer. Ideally all of them should have an assessment by a mental health professional as a minimum. Treatment requires special skills and training and within departments of psychology and child psychiatry, where these resources are often concentrated, there is a greater demand than can be met.

Without therapeutic help children who have been abused run the risk of abusing their own children and thus completing the cycle. Whilst we know that there are survivors who through their own resources cope with the effects of early abuse, the outlook is likely to be much better with appropriate therapy. However this takes time and resources and an expansion in these services is urgently required.

Finally there was a newspaper story reported recently of the 16-year-old girl who gave birth to her full-term 6lb baby 'by the light of a street lamp in her bedroom'. She hid the baby's body in several plastic bags in a locker in school where it was discovered seven weeks later. Only then did the girl admit she was the mother. The coroner expressed astonishment that the girl had gone through the ordeal alone. Detective Inspector Cousins asked 'How on earth can a young girl go to school for nine months and it not be known that she is pregnant?' The girl was described as 'an extremely frightened young lady' at the time of the birth. The family solicitor described the parents as dedicated and loving. The police said no charges would be pressed against the girl but refused to say what had happened to the baby's father. The parents say with hindsight that they had their suspicions but never pushed her into admitting it.

The solicitor said 'all families could learn from the case'. 'Parents need to try to be more open and honest with their children and share with them the fears and strains of being a teenager'. These particular parents would very much like to be more open and honest with their child.

In this apparently enlightened age of sexual openness this case raises some interesting questions. Child abuse exists widely in society and our awareness continues to grow. There are signs that it is beginning to be debated more openly. Recognition of the signs and symptoms that a child is being abused is an essential starting point to any effort to help.

Appendix 1.1

Child sexual abuse Pre and Post Cleveland

	1985/6	1989
Confirmed/probable cases	337	237
Mean age	8.0	6.9
% five years	38%	41%
% boys	28%	28%
% case conference held	67%	64%
% conference register CSA	86%	62%
% cases register CSA	57%	41%
Admission in to care	36%	24%
Perpetrator convicted	17%	5%

(Frothingham and others, 1993)

References

American Academy of Paediatrics (Committee on child abuse and neglect) (1991) 'Guidelines for the evaluation of sexual abuse of children' *Paediatrics* 87 (2), 254-259

Branch, G and Paxton, RA (1965) 'A study of gonococcal infection amongst infants and children', *Public Health Report*, 80, 347-352

Buchanan and Oliver (1979) Abuse and neglect as a cause of mental retardation, *Child Abuse and Neglect*, 3, 467-475

Corwin, DL, Wyatt, GE and Powell GJ (eds) (1988) 'Early diagnosis of child sexual abuse: diminishing the lasting effects', *Lasting effects of Child Sexual Abuse*. Sage

Frothingham, TE, and others (1993) 'Child abuse before and after Cleveland', *Child Abuse Review*, 2, 23-34

Hanks, HGI and Hobbs, CJ (1993) Failure to thrive – a model for treatment. *in* Hobbs, CJ and Wynne JM (eds) *Bailliere's Clinical Paediatrics, Child Abuse*. Balliere Tindall, 101-119

Hobbs, CJ and Wynne JM (eds) (1993) *Bailliere's Clinical Paediatrics, Child Abuse*, 1, 1(Feb). Bailliere Tindall

Hobbs, CJ, Hanks HGI, Wynne, JM (1993) *Child abuse and neglect -a clinician's handbook*. Churchill Livingstone

Hobbs, CJ and Wynne JM (1990) 'The sexually abused battered child', *Archives of Disease in Childhood*, 65, 423-427

Kennedy, M (1990) 'No more secrets', *Deafness Journal*, 6(1), 10-12

Muram, D, Speck, PM and Gould, SS (1991) 'Genital abnormalities in female siblings and friends of child victims of sexual abuse', *Child Abuse & Neglect*, 15, 105-110

Royal College of Physicans (1991) *Physical signs of sexual abuse of children.*

Sinason, V (1993) 'The vulnerability of the handicapped child and adult: with special reference to mental handicap' (learning disability). *in* Hobbs, CJ and Wynne JM (eds) *Balliere's Clinical Paediatrics, Child Abuse*, 69-86

Summit, RC (1983) 'The child sexual abuse accommodation syndrome', *Child Abuse and Neglect* 7, 177-193

2. Exploring the tensions between partnership, protection and prevention in early years services

Margy Whalley, Head
Pen Green Centre, Corby

As early years educators, we are all aware that the education and care of children under five is complimentary and inseparable (DES, 1988), and that early years workers wanting to provide the highest quality service need to work creatively with parents, care givers and the community. This was not always the case.

Child protection is a recurring theme in the history of early years services but those with the power to make decisions about levels of service provision have always had ambivalent views about both the appropriateness of intervening in the life of the family for the sake of the child; and about the nature of the intervention, that is, whether the state intervenes to enable all children to have an equal start through universal state education or whether the state should intervene to protect particular children from their 'feckless parents'. (Prevention of cruelty to, and protection of, Children Act 1889).

Ambivalence

Even serious reformers like Shaftesbury saw compulsory education 'as an infringement of the parent's right to bring up the child as he saw fit, and as encouraging undesirable dependence on the state'. (Fox-Harding 1991).

A Court in 1878 could state that, 'the right of the father to the custody and control of his child is one of the most sacred of rights'.

Some charitable organisations in Britain in the second half of the 19th century held the view that:

'It is better in the interests of the community to allow the sins of the parents to be visited on the children, than to impair the principle of the solidarity of the family and run the risk of permanently demoralising large numbers of the population by offering free meals to their children.' (Pinchbeck and Hewitt, 1969)

In the 1990s it is always important to take a European perspective. One of the parents who manages the centre where I work and who had recently visited a Danish 0 to 14 provision, reflected that we were still stuffing children up chimneys in England when the Danes were setting up recreation services for all their children.

This defence of the birth family, the belief that the sanctity of the family should not be disturbed except in extreme circumstances is *one constant* in the great confusion over whether or not public services should be provided for our youngest children.

Although families, and specifically mothers, have consistently demonstrated a desire and a need for education and care services for children under five, they were largely unheard. The only exceptions to this were during times of war when women were needed in the workforce and the state 'decided that children could do without their mothers in the interests of the nation' (David, 1990). Some of the youngest children even attended residential day nurseries, only returning to their parents at weekends (Webb, 1991; Riley, 1983).

Like the Headstart programme in the US in the 1960s, initial government drives to increase early years provision were very much influenced by the fact that large numbers of recruits (approximately 60 per cent in Britain in the 1900s) were unfit for military service. In the departmental committee on physical deterioration (1903–1904) there was anxiety that Britain would become a 'C3' nation, that is, belonging to the lowest army medical classification (Fox-Harding, 1991). One speaker in the 1905 parliamentary debate stated that 'care for children was good economy and good imperialism' (Fox-Harding, 1991).

Increasingly, the state did intervene; the 1908 Children Act and the 1933 Children and Young Persons Act both elaborated the powers of the state and legitimised state intervention which focused initially on childrens' physical well-being. By the 1960s state intervention was geared up to supporting socially deprived families who had fallen through the safety net of the welfare state (1963 Children and Young Persons Act) and the psychological and emotional needs of children were being addressed.

The concept of nursery education as a right for all children was not addressed however and Margaret McMillen's concept of nursery education as a liberating and politicising force was also lost.

It is important to understand this historical perspective that is, 'where services come from', since most of the tensions we are forced to address in the family centre I manage are as a consequence of these persistent warring ideologies between the role of state and the family, warring ideologies about motherhood; about the child's need for care or the child's need for education, and the need to reconcile the tension 'between child care agents of the state, intervening too much, too coercively and about them doing too little, too ineffectually' (Fox-Harding, 1991).

Reconciling the need to both protect children and also to protect innocent families from unnecessary intervention by the state (Prime Minister quoted in Oliver, 1988) would imply that legislation and policy are trying to go in two different directions at once, leaving social workers, health workers and early childhood educators effectively paralysed and not knowing where their responsibility lies. In the case of the Orkneys, Cleveland and Nottingham, social workers were perceived as acting too hastily, but in individual child abuse 'scandals' and enquiries social work intervention is often seen as too little and too late.

The Children Act (1989) enshrines the principle of non-intervention in family life (Children Act 1989 Section I). This principle in the Act states that courts should not make orders with regard to a child unless it considers it better for the child than making no order at all – (Fox-Harding, 1991). The Children Act legislation also reflects the kind of tensions which are experienced daily in many families.

The 'parental responsibility versus children's rights' debate is value based and reflects very specific and cultural mores. Parents living in poverty or with their backs against the wall are put into double bind positions. I call this the 'Families can't win syndrome'.

- Stay with an abusive partner, brownie points for holding family together.

  Children become distressed, aggressive or withdrawn. Leave partner – live in hostel or refuge, children distressed.

- Living in a hostel for the homeless, brownie points for keeping one room tidy which moves you up the housing list.

  Children have to watch videos and 'be good'.

- Parents live in houses without fences or hedges. Parks vandalised, brownie points for keeping children safely inside.

  Children stay inside, angry or apathetic.

- Parents, particularly single parents can't afford babysitters or dare not leave child with babysitters. Brownie points for staying at home.

  Parents become depressed, isolated or leave child unattended or inappropriately attended.

- Parents want to work for financial reward or personal fulfilment but there is no nursery or day care provision. Brownie points for staying at home and being a 'good mother' and 'leaving jobs for those that really need them'.

  Parent ends up feeling trapped, depressed, maybe fails to meet the needs of his/her child and ends up in a family centre where professionals share the care of the children (child care is what they wanted in the first place!)

Early years services have to offer a balanced provision which respects both the rights of children and the *rights* of parents. Early years services also need to be clear where parental responsibilities begin and end. David Willetts, formerly Director of Studies of the

Centre for Policy Studies and now Conservative MP for Havant, 'regards the decision to have a child as the same as any other spending decision in these days of contraception. It is the same as deciding to buy a CD player or a car. It is entirely a personal matter' (Melhuish and Moss, 1991). From this perspective it is easy to see how just as contraception remains largely the province and responsibility of women, then so must the care and education of children remain largely the province and responsibility of women. Early years services from this viewpoint are seen as purely reactive services for those families who are unable to cope. Parents at the centre call this the 'you have to bang your child on the head to get any support' approach.

The Children Act (1989) does however open up the possibilities for a more liberal perspective by outlining the duty of local authorities to provide a range and level of services appropriate to children in need. The Act's failure to define unambiguously 'a child in need' and the fact that there has been no significant increase in resourcing children's services means that a child defined as in need and receiving support in one local authority might not even qualify for a day care place in another. In point of fact a child in need in one town within a local authority might receive an entirely different level of service provision from a child living less than 10 miles away, such is the muddle and confusion within early years services (Whalley, 1993).

Pen Green Centre for under fives and their families was set up in 1983 to be a holistic service to children and families, balancing the needs of parents and children. The service was to be pro-active in terms of providing a wide range of services to all families that wanted to use them within a specific catchment area, and re-active in that provision could be offered to targeted children that is, those on the child protection register or where there was real cause for concern.

The centre was located in a neighbourhood where there was a high incidence of factors commonly associated with the social/welfare problems that lead to family stress. Philosophically it stemmed from a review of provision for under fives in the country which would reflect the need for a 'type of provision which aims to provide stimulating opportunities for child development, plus day care, plus the need for compensatory provision (and consequent relief for the mother)' (Northamptonshire County Council Report 1976).

The principles underpinning the service were that it was to be locally based with open access to young families. Vulnerable groups were to be targeted in particular, for example, single parents, teenage parents, parents with mental health problems and so on. Family support services were to be established that did not 'pathologise' families and thus encourage 'clients status'. The community social work model that was to be adopted required staff to draw on the strengths within families and the community at large. Parents were to be encouraged to share their 'complimentary expertise' in caring for their children rather than being presented with a 'professional model' of 'appropriate care'. They were to be encouraged to use welfare services appropriately and wherever possible to become 'service providers'. This was consistent with the social services department's principles for service delivery: 'to help people help themselves ..... to promote independence, to avoid dependency.' (Hiscock, July 1987)

It was set up as a reaction against the kind of family support model where one 'client' might have to relate to any number of professional workers. One parent, **Kate**, for example, was put in touch with:

clinical nurse manager	community psychiatric nurse
health visitor	psychiatrist
NSPCC	police
social workers	probation
teachers	children's centre staff
education welfare officers	housing welfare
child and family guidance	welfare rights
clinical medical officer	Department of Social Security
unit manager health	district nurse
(Hep B Clinic)	
GP	

Instead parents could use the centre in their way and in their own time. For example, **Jane** came into the centre as a 16-year-old teenager completing a work placement in an office. She got pregnant, married, had a child and then two more. At 19 she was involved in Open University groups. Her first night out after her first baby was born was to attend the course on babies and toddlers. She started using the baby clinic where health visitors counselled, volunteers made coffee, parents used the digital scales to weigh their babies and spent the afternoon chatting and exchanging news. She joined a women's support group and disclosed the fact that she had been abused and subsequently joined a women's survivors group. She attended a writer's group on a Monday evening and her children attended the evening creche which was available. Jane's children were offered consistent child care through a nurture group for children under three and in the community nursery.

Ellen is a parent with three children. In 1983 more than half the parents attending the centre were bringing up children on their own as she was. In 1993 many of the families using the centre are now re-constituted families. Each of Ellen's children had a different father. Ellen used the baby clinic initially and attended the 'drop-in' approximately 25 hours a week. She had been the victim of domestic violence in her previous relationships and her current partner was also abusive. Ellen wanted individual counselling and got it, attended a mixed gender group which explored relationships within families and also attended a contact group looking at contact between her three children, their three fathers and all their different sets of grandparents. Her Christmas Day schedule for instance was a nightmare since there was an expectation that each child would spend time with their grandparents. Her children needed counselling and consistent child care so that they could find a voice for their anger and pain and so that they could be heard.

'The power relations between adults and children are all wrong..... they must be changed so adults would no longer be convinced of their right to arrange the life and world of the child as *they* think best, without considering the child's feelings about it.' Janusz Korczak (in Bettelheim, 1990).

Alan, a single parent father living in a hostel for the homeless, did not want to be a 'client' of the social services department. He had lost his house but not his pride. He had given up work to look after his children when his partner left him and was extremely competent. He did not want women workers or parents taking over his parenting role nor did he want to attend the men's group which was on offer. He needed somewhere to come out to where he could do his laundry. He also was deeply committed to his children's education and was very interested in their intellectual development. He joined the parents in the nursery group, attended training days with an early years consultant, maintained wonderful records of the patterns in his children's play, helped out in the nursery and was respected and valued by nursery staff.

In a community based centre like ours working with the education and care needs of children and offer a variety of services to parents including adult education (GCSEs and 'A' levels) community education, therapeutic groups, self-help groups and toy libraries, and so on, we meet a cross section of the families within our community. Parents are sometimes in extremely stressful situations, in Holloway prison, in a psychiatric hospital, with children in care and there are also parents coping with everyday pressures of shiftwork, three children under five, a child with special needs or parents just feeling overwhelmed with the responsibilities of bringing up a child. Children's interests are paramount but we want to offer support to parents and to meet their needs as well. In child protection terms, parents who feel listened to, parents who are encouraged to question, challenge, make choices and deal constructively with some of the nightmares they may have experienced in thier own lives, go on to be parents who are much better able to listen to and protect their children. Children who have a positive self image, who are encouraged to be assertive, to challenge, question and choose are, I believe, less likely to be abused, or at the very least better able to deal with the consequences of abuse (see Figure 2.1).

How effective are we?

We constantly need to ask ourselves whether we could provide a better service to children and their families and since all the staff have backgrounds in different disciplines we are aware of some gaps in our training.

- Teachers are expected to listen to children and hear them tell of abuse without appropriate training or support. Teachers are very frightened of making mistakes, hence the reduction in referrals to child protection agencies (David, 1993).
- Social workers are expected to identify children in need when

Figure 2.1 Children's needs and parents' needs

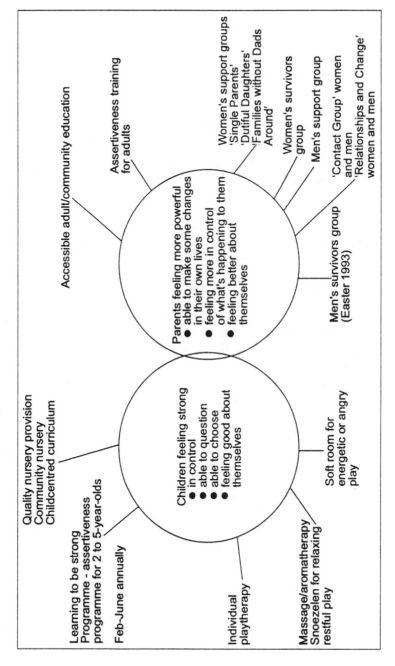

there is little in their training on normal child development. They also fear getting it wrong.

- Health workers have little preparation on their courses for dealing with the consequence of a disclosure and may get little support from GPs who are also afraid. They may well receive minimal supervision, and often have no training for court work. With GP fund holding many health visitors are being pulled out of community work.

There is a real need for multidisciplinary training in child protection and in working with children and families, and funding **must** be made available for it.

As workers who provide services to families, we want to be friends to children and resourceful friends to their parents, but what we need is a society which values **all** of its children and makes appropriate provision for them.

References

David, T (1993) *Child protection and early years teachers: coping with child abuse.* Open University Press

David, T (1990) *Under five – under education.* Open University Press

Department for Education (1990) *Starting with quality.* Report of the Committee of Inquiry into the quality of the educational experience offered to 3-4 year olds. Rumbold Report

Department of Health (1991) *Guidance & regulations vol.2. Family support day care and educational provision for young children.* HMSO

Fox Harding, L (1991) *Perspectives in childcare policy.* Longman

Korczak, J. *in* Bettleheim, B (1990) *Recollections and Reflections.* Thames & Hudson

Melhuish, EC and Moss, P (1991) *Daycare for young children – international perspectives.* Routledge

Northants County Council (1976) *Provision for the under fives in Northamptonshire.*

Oliver, J (1983) 'Introducing the Children Bill', *Social Work Today.* December

Pinchbeck, I and Hewitt, M (1969) *Children in English Society.* Routledge, Kegan Paul

Riley, K (1983) *War in the nursery: Theories of the child and mother.* Virago

Webb, J (1991) 'Forgotten years', *Early Years,* vol 12, pp8-13

Whalley, M (1993) *Learning to be strong. Setting up a neighbourhood service for under fives and families.* Hodder & Stoughton

3. Strategies for building a multidisciplinary reponse in the context of the Children Act

Rob Sykes, Director of Operations
Oxfordshire Social Services

Introduction

The early childhood services have three main roles in relation to child protection:

- prevention or (more helpfully) the promotion of the welfare of children in need;
- recognition of abuse;
- monitoring as part of a treatment programme.

This paper is based on the premise that it is a self evident pre-requisite of a strategy for child protection that there should be a clear and robust strategy for the development of early years services generally. Integral to this strategy must be the development of clear standards of quality. It is only within this context that it is possible to look at issues about recognition of monitoring and abuse.

Background – children's services

Figure 3.1 is a diagrammatic representation of how children in need could/should be dealt with by a social services department. The important thing is that only those cases where it is absolutely necessary should be dealt with by social workers/care managers (A). Even then as much use as possible should be made of general resources (B).

Figure 3.1   Social services for children in need

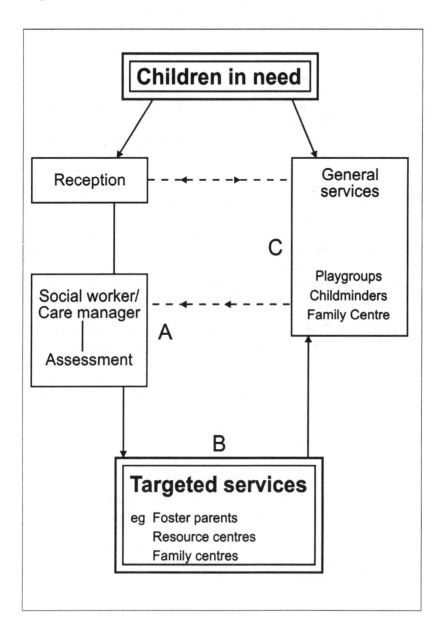

As often as possible people should be re-directed to general services (C) and this requires this sector to be strong.

In modern jargon the commissioning issue is how much money to put into 'A', 'B' or 'C'. In many authorities the increasing resource intensity of 'A' means there is little money left for the promotion of welfare yet lack of spending on general service may lead to increased demand in social worker/care manager intervention. In addition, in my work with the Audit Commission, it has become clear that there are still authorities where social workers have little or no budget for spending on flexible packages to prevent reception into care.

I believe standards in child protection should be high but I think we have got to the point where the benefits of continuing to make this service more and more time intensive must be weighed against the gains of developing general services.

Figures 3.2 and 3.3 show that spending on children's services has actually remained constant since 1986 at a time when the number of children in care has dropped dramatically and the numbers in residential care even more so. My thesis (which needs to be checked) would be that the resulting money saved has in the main gone in making child protection standards higher and higher (for example it is not uncommon for the legal costs in a particular case to be £100,000 without social work time). The time may have come to question whether that trend should continue. Clearly child protection work should be funded properly and to reasonable standards but the benefits from continually increasing the time taken on individual cases must now be questioned so that a proper balance between services which promote welfare and those which are reactive can be maintained.

Developing a strategy for under eights

The development of playgroups, childminders and day care is therefore key in a comprehensive children's strategy. Figure 3.4 shows in Oxfordshire 51 per cent of the provision is playgroups and 30 per cent childminders. Obviously other authorities may have more nursery provision but the significance of playgroups and childminders cannot be underestimated.

Figure 3.2 Real changes in children expenditure

% of budget spent on children, % of population under 18

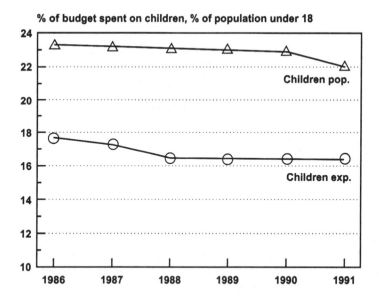

Performance Information Unit - March 1993

Figure 3.3 Children in care at 31 March 1980 to 1990, England

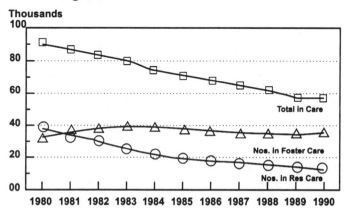

Performance Information Unit - March 1993

Figure 3.4   Actual places by type of provision, Oxfordshire

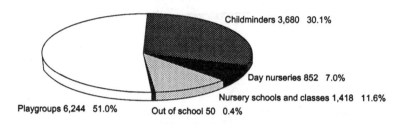

Childminders 3,680   30.1%

Day nurseries 852   7.0%

Nursery schools and classes 1,418   11.6%

Playgroups 6,244   51.0%   Out of school 50   0.4%

Performance Information Unit – March 1993

How do you put together a strategy that brings together education/social services and thousands of independent providers. Figure 3.5 shows how we have attempted to do it in Oxfordshire. The important points are:

- a strategic group which brings together education/social services/independent sector;
- local groups doing several things:

  — giving information on local priorities to the strategic group;
  — identifying gaps;
  — spending money on joint training.

This gives you a proper base to undertake the review required under the Children Act and enables local consultation on what parents and providers are actually saying is needed. In Oxfordshire we undertook a range of consultation meetings in each area. It also gives a good basis for local training and close working relations between social services/education staff and local providers. It is worth noting that there now exist models for looking at an authority and identifying ward by ward where the greatest deprivation exists and therefore where facilities for children in need should be targeted.

I think it is worth concentrating for a moment on the role of family centres. The first difficulty is that the words mean everything

Figure 3.5   Divisional liaison panels

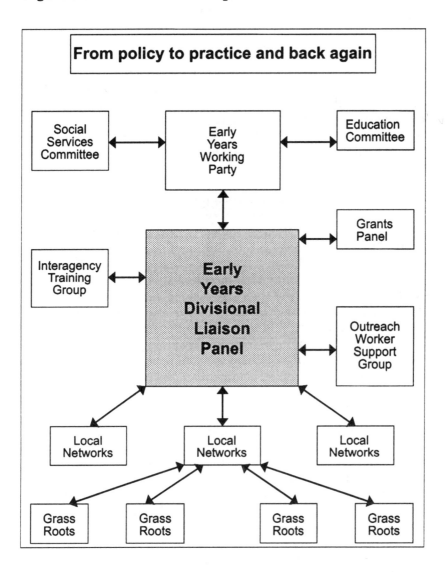

Performance Information Unit – February 1993

to everybody. They range from highly targeted facilities taking only referred cases to totally open drop-in facilities.

Clearly there is a need for the whole spectrum of services, the problem is how should they be delivered? In Oxfordshire we had to cope with the added difficulty of a county with some urban centres and a large rural hinterland. We have gone for a model of developing family centres in selected urban areas which will take referred cases but which provide outreach and general services. In the rural areas we concentrate on providing support and assistance to general provision. We also have a network of sponsored childminders who are paid a special rate and who receive particular training to take referred cases.

The debate about what is a family centre is unlikely to ever be resolved but I would like to focus on one issue of concern from my work with the Audit Commission. In at least one authority we have seen a family centre strategy which is purely about 'heavy end' referred cases. That is the choice they have made and although it is not my choice, for them, it is logical. However the staff who are involved in this service, which is intended to be intensive/therapeutic, are all from what was their day nursery service. The lesson for me is be clear what the Centre's role is and make sure the job specifications, training and so on equip the staff to fulfil that role. On the issue of support, we employ psychologists who undertake sessions at family centres to help the staff develop programmes for groups and parents.

Standards in day care

Volume 2 of the Children Act guidance (Department of Health, 1991) included regulations about floor space, staff ratios, attitudes to equal opportunities and ability to care for children. I thought the standards were reasonable. In Oxfordshire we were clear at the time of implementation that we didn't want to reduce the amount of day care and we therefore had a policy of implementing the guidance as flexibly as possible. For example, we would give time for compliance on toilets, training and so on and no facility would be refused registration without reference to a senior officer. Money was made available for grants for families and to the Preschool Playgroups Association to provide training. We give £190,000 pa to the PPA and part of this pays for replacement staff for people going on courses.

We had three complaints from 3,000 registrations. The PPA wrote to Ministers saying what a good experience they had in Oxfordshire. One of the complainants wrote to a national newspaper and was subsequently on TV. It was probably pressure from groups like this that led to the DOH 'clarifying' their guidance (Department of Health, 1993).

As with all these things the situation was more complicated than the story told, for example the fact that the Inspector had found unguarded heaters and children were not washing their hands when they had been to the toilet because of the lack of facilities. The place was called a nursery school but we couldn't verify the Head's qualifications. I am *not* suggesting this was a poor facility, just that there were issues that merited a close look!

In the same article a provider says she has been asked to provide stairgates. She said 'I have never used stairgates, I use something called discipline'. I leave you to make your own judgement on that.

The line I took with the TV at the time was that I think parents want to be assured they are buying a reasonable standard of care and I am sure the press would pick it up if anything went wrong.

My concern is that the legal advice we have had is that the new circular makes it almost impossible to enforce some standards. How flexible is flexible? We are asking our Committee to back us on continuing with the Children Act guidance on staffing ratios until the planned DOH review. But we may well see the courts defining standards in the coming months.

In the context of this paper I have to mention the circular's insistence that criminal record checks should not be undertaken on voluntary playgroups, day nurseries and so on. Because there is less scope for one to one contact with children in a group setting, most convicted offenders are men and most day care workers are women.

Compare that with the Warner Report's insistence on police checking in children's homes!

The American experience is that unregulated day care is poor day care. The National Child Care Staffing Study in a study of 227 day centres in five cities found that in the majority of centres care was rated as barely adequate with staff turnover at 41 per cent per year (Whitebook and others, 1990).

I would contend that we need reasonable standards which can be enforced for three reasons:

- to prevent abusive environments developing;
- to provide good quality facilities which promote welfare and lessen the effects of deprivation;
- to ensure that staff are able to recognise children at risk and take appropriate action.

I hope local authorities will continue to set and maintain reasonable standards and I hope if there are court cases, this stance will be supported.

The Area Child Protection Committee

Figure 3.6 sets out the structure of the ACPC in Oxfordshire with sub groups on training and prevention. It is imperative that the ACPC links with key workers in the under eight's field to ensure a number of minimum standards are in place:

- basic training is available for childminders, playgroups staff and so on. which includes guidance about what to do if they are concerned about a child in their care;
- leaflets are available to the same group of people;
- key staff such as inspectors and early years staff in education are targeted for more comprehensive training so they know what to do if they are asked advice;
- clear procedures for health visitors, training in recognition and time to attend conferences.

In addition there are a number of general child protection issues which are particularly relevant to young children:

- are there joint interviewing protocols with the police? Are there proper child friendly facilities? Are staff specially trained?
- Are there arrangements to avoid repeat interviewing and medical?
- Is there a treatment strategy which includes facilities for young children for example, play therapists and so on.

As recent publicity has shown, there is a key issue about recognition

Figure 3.6 ACPC committee and working groups

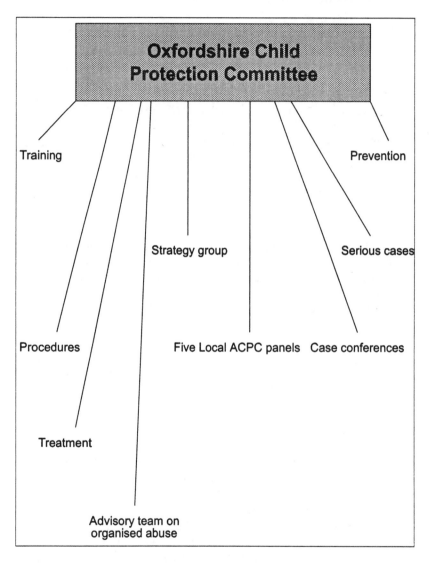

of abuse in children with special needs. This needs special attention because of communication difficulties.

The organisational link between child protection and under eight's

This is a plea that as departments become more specialist the link between these two areas of work is maintained for two reasons:

- the availability of general preventative resources will be dependent on the under eight's workers;
- good working relationships will ensure that cases which are recognised are dealt with appropriately. The dangers of over reaction as well as lack of action will be avoided.

Summary

- Child protection cannot be seen outside the context of the development of a strategy for under eight's which sets and maintains clear standards. There must be a balance between a general service which promotes welfare and heavy end services for those on the child protection register.
- Information and training must be available to a wide variety of staff so that children who may be the subject of abuse are recognised and dealt with appropriately.
- General as well as specialist services can have a key role in monitoring and treatment programmes for children on the child protection register but the staff need adequate training and support.

References

Department of Health (1991), *The Children Act 1989 Guidance and Regulations, Volume 2: Family Support, Day Care and Educational Provision for Young Children.* HMSO
Department of Health (1993) *The Children Act and Day Care for Young Children: Registration.* LAC (93) 1, HMSO
Whitebook, M, Howes C and Phillips (1990) *Who Cares? Child Care Teachers and Quality of Care in America.* Executive Summary of National Child Care Strategies Study.

Workshops

4. Developing a child protection training strategy for early years workers

Anne Hollows and Jane Wonnacott
Child Abuse Training Unit, National Children's Bureau

The keynote papers highlight the vital part played by early years workers in preventing the abuse of young children. Where abuse nevertheless occurs, the papers indicate the importance of early years workers being able to recognise the symptoms and signs and to respond to young children who have been abused. These roles are demanding. Both training and professional support are essential if workers are to be able to work effectively with the children and families in their care. Training should enable staff to feel more confident in their knowledge and skills and more able to ensure that what they see and hear from children and their parents is shared within the professional network. This is particularly important for early years workers whose contribution to child protection conferences is often marginalised.

The key issues in developing effective child protection training for early years workers seem to be as follows:

- embedding the training strategy clearly in Area Child Protection Committee polices;
- Identifying training needs;
- Thinking creatively about ways of meeting the training needs and deciding who will implement the programme;
- Setting up effective evaluation.

Embedding the strategy in ACPC policy

Early years workers come from a variety of agencies and include those who are privately funded, such as playgroups and childminders. If they are all to receive effective training there needs to be a coordinated, inter-agency approach to planning and delivering the training. In some authorities there will be a committee dealing with under eight's issues which will include representatives from social work, education and health and such a committee would need to consider these issues. The Area Child Protection Committee is the obvious arena common to all parts of the country in which such a training strategy should be debated and most ACPCs have a multi agency training sub group set up for such a purpose. Not all training will need to be delivered in a multi-agency forum, but there should be some clarity about which aspects of training should be developed by single agencies and which should be organised on a multi-agency basis.

ACPCs will need, first, to acknowledge the fundamental role which early years services play in the prevention of abuse and the protection of children. Clarity about the need to develop effective services for the under eights will enable member agencies of the ACPC to set service objectives for those which feed into the development of a coordinated training strategy.

If training is varied from this angle, agencies should find that there can be some time and resource savings as the duplication of effort is minimised. For example, it too may be that training materials can be developed that are applicable across a variety of staff groups. Workers in family centres, playgroups, nursery classes and paediatric wards may train together and gain strength from discussing the similarity of the situations being faced in a variety of settings.

If the evaluation of these training activities is fed back through to the ACPC, policy makers may have a clearer idea of the way in which policy and procedures need to be developed to make best use of the expertise that resides in those who work on a daily basis with small children.

Identifying training needs

The training needs of early years workers in relation to child protection will vary between staff groups and individuals. In identifying need, the knowledge, skills and attitudes required should be identified and gaps for individuals and/or teams highlighted. For example, a teacher in a nursery class may need, (among other things):

- knowledge of risk factors;
- the indicators of abuse;
- local procedures;
- skills in communicating with children about abuse;
- an understanding of the attitudes and values they bring to their work.

In the early years field, those responsible for identifying training needs and nominating staff for training events may not be those with knowledge of child protection issues. In the case of private playgroups and childminders it may be that the person responsible for registration will be the key to analysing need and ensuring that appropriate training is undertaken.

If they are not given training in the issues around child protection, it is unlikely that they will be able to correctly analyse need or ensure that the right training is reaching the right people. Clarity is needed about who in each agency is responsible for identifying the child protection training needs of early years workers. It is all too easy for specialist child protection trainers to assume that early years specialists know about child protection, and vice versa. Here, again, an ACPC which is effectively developing and monitoring training across all agencies can be of vital help.

Fulfilling training needs

All too often, training is seen as being synonymous with a training course. A more flexible approach to training can be helpful for many staff, but particularly those who find difficulty in being released from the workplace for long periods.

Many early years workers are in this category. Where a training course is important staff should not be denied the opportunity of attending, but an essential training course *plus* other training methods can provide a richer experience. Other methods may include observation sessions, job swaps with other professionals, working alongside a more experienced worker, discussions in staff meetings and time for private study.

In planning courses the timing will need to be carefully considered in relation to work settings and the possible additional costs of this accounted for. Childminders may prefer evenings, and there will be other examples.

When delivering a training event around child protection it is always important to consider the emotional impact that the material may have on participants. It is likely that some participants will themselves be survivors of abuse and may need support through the training event. Other staff will recognise, during training, the situations in the past which they failed to identify child protection issues. Many early years workers may be going back to an isolated work situation with little ongoing support and they may benefit from an opportunity to follow up any training in terms of the impact it has had on them.

It will be essential also to engage the managers or supervisors of staff attending training. While training can begin the process of developing knowledge and skills, it will not alone change working competencies. Staff will need to be able to refine and develop the skills they have started to learn on the course. They will also need to have the means to update their knowledge after the training. Their continuing progress along a learning curve is an essential part of their developing response to child protection issues in their working environment.

Evaluation

Evaluation of training involves a combination of activities which, taken together will demonstrate the effectiveness of a training programme. It will need to consider whether the correct training needs for early years workers were identified and whether these were appropriately matched to individuals and groups of staff. It will need to consider the way in which the content of the training and the form of training was appropriate to the overall goals which were identified. Were the right staff selected with the right previous experience? The quality of the training itself, its delivery and the way in which the training group functioned will also be matters for consideration. After training it will be important to consider the assistance provided in the workplace to putting the training into practice. Finally it will be necessary to assess what changes in child protection practice resulted from the training. Evaluation is the means of keeping the training wheel turning: each evaluation will generate new demands for training and should improve its targeting and effectiveness. It should also provide a consistent means of charting the development of child protection services in the early years.

5. Observation, assessment and support: the contribution of early years workers

Dorothy Rouse, Development Officer,
Early Childhood Unit, National Children's Bureau
Olivia Vincenti
Curtis Family Centre, Barnet

This workshop was planned to think about the role of teachers, playgroup leaders, parents, group day care workers, family day care workers and other educators in protecting children from abuse, as well as working to heal children who have been abused.

To set the scene for the activity, I want to introduce two themes and begin to explore some questions arising from them.

- To explore the role of teachers and other educators from two perspectives:

  — Educators are often left out of multi professional work ... why?
  — Educators must be integrated into multi professional teams ... why?

- To think about the importance of observation and assessment in child protection work. What do educators need to know and do so that they can develop more confidence and competence in observing and assessing children?
  What can other professionals expect and what do they need from educators to support their work with abused children?

Why are teachers left out?

Teachers, local education authorities, and other educarers are relieved to be *out of the media spotlight* when child abuse is exposed and analysed in the press. If something were to 'go wrong' and children were the subject of local or national notoriety then schools and nurseries would be relieved not to have their carefully developed *relationship of trust and confidence with parents and the community jeopardised.*

Traditionally, teachers and other educators are often only involved with social workers, health visitors, child guidance and hospital personnel *when something is wrong.* This kind of working relationship means they don't have a positive basis in their work which helps them to trust one another to initiate programmes of assessment or intervention for children in their care. Often educators are possessive about 'their' children in 'their' nursery, working with 'their' parents and muddled about the confidentiality aspects of supporting children who have been abused.

Sometimes educators may wait for overwhelming evidence of abuse to emerge before contacting social services rather than airing their worries at an earlier stage because they are afraid that children will be removed from the continuity of care within the school or nursery in favour of therapeutic treatment outside the catchment area. Educators need to be able to trust their colleagues and share responsibility with them for making decisions so they can draw on each other's expertise. Conversely they may find it so painful to be dealing daily with abusive families and neglected or abused children they may long for their 'problem' to be removed and be the responsibility of some other professional.

In either case these situations indicate a need for supervision and support for educators. Supervision and support is well established for staff working in day care and social services. Teachers do not have a formal structure for exploring hunches, sharing worries or interpreting their observations with a supportive colleague. Of course many head teachers do have a 'my door is always open – you can come and discuss anything, anytime' policy, but in my experience this is not the same as formal supervision with regular structured opportunities for self assessment, evaluation of work programmes or support for planning the curriculum.

Teachers views may be seen as ineffectual because they are

believed to have shallow everyday group contact rather than inti-
mate and personal interviews with the child and family. This pre-
supposes that social workers and health visitors may have a narrow
view of the teachers role in school; that of imparting knowledge and
whole class subject teaching rather than being concerned with the
child's holistic learning needs, including their need to explore a
range of feelings and to develop assertiveness skills.

Teachers do have primary concern for cognitive development
and often other professionals do perceive that educators have a
lesser concern for observations and assessment of children's emotional learning and this may be another reason why educators are
left out of child protection work.

Wattam (1990) identifies three impediments to teachers reporting suspected abuse which could mean teachers views are not
sought or respected.

* A refusal to believe that abuse really happens. For example this
  teacher is wondering about whether abuse is really happening:

  'It is difficult for schools to deal with more 'iffy' things ...
  children seem so sexualised. It is television and video we'd never
  seen in our day? When I played house I made tea, not babies. You
  see them humping about in the home corner and wonder where
  they have learnt about adult sexual behaviour. Does it mean
  someone has been abused?'
  (Frances *in* David, 1993)

Do educators, (or any of us) have a problem in distinguishing
between 'normal' childlike sexual curiosity and inappropriate sexual behaviour?

* Sexual abuse is a particularly difficult type of abuse for teachers
  to deal with in a society which is permeated with restrictions
  and taboos about discussing sex or private and confidential
  matters openly.
* Many educators would have difficulty in discussing or reporting their observations of children's sexual behaviour. In some
  schools and nurseries this is a taboo subject.

The difficulty of accepting that short term damage caused by referral may actually be less traumatic in the long run compared to the effects of abuse of a child by an adult.

The longer term effects of trauma are explicitly described by this child in an autobiographical novel.

> 'I didn't daydream (while masturbating) about fire anymore. Now I imagined people watching while Daddy Glen beat me, though only when it was not happening. I screamed and kicked and cried like the baby I was. But sometimes when I was safe and alone, I would imagine the ones who watched. Someone had to watch - some girl I admired who barely knew I existed, some girl from church or down the street, or one of my cousins, or even somebody I had seen on television. Sometimes a whole group of them would be trapped into watching. They couldn't help or get away. They had to watch. In my imagination I was proud and defiant. I'd stare back at him with my teeth set, making no sound at all, no shameful scream, no begging. I pictured it that way and put my hands between my legs. It was scary, but it was thrilling too. Those who watched me, loved me. It was as if I was being beaten for them. I was wonderful in their eyes.' (p 112, Allison, 1993)
>
> 'Lying alone on the big bed, I thought about Daddy Glen and the way he would come up behind me and gather me up in his arms to pull me close to his body. Remembering, I locked my hands between my legs and tightened every muscle in my body. When I was as hard and rigid as I could make myself, I tried to remember how it started. What was it I had done? Why had he always hated me? Maybe I was a bad girl, evil, nasty, wilful, stupid, ugly - everything he said. Maybe I was, but it didn't matter. I hated him, and these days I even hated Reese (her sister) and Mama. I was a bowl of hatred, boiling black and thick behind my eyes.' (p 252, Allison, 1993)

Do educators shy away from the horror of this kind of trauma as they are more closely concerned with the discontinuity in children's care and education or because they want to pass on a painful issue?

Educators are also left out because of their own professional low self esteem and their low status in the hierarchy of child care and health professionals. Early years teachers, nursery nurses and other educators in playgroups and nurseries work with the youngest children and are unjustly often considered by many as having low professional status. Many early years workers have low salaries and inadequate training for the work that they do. Other professionals do not therefore accord them equal respect for their experience or expertise in working with young children. Other professionals may not seek or value teachers observations or interventions in working with young children who have been abused.

The advantages of integrating teachers into the professional team

Teachers have daily contact with children

Early years educators are frequently seen by their pupils as someone who cares about them and someone whom they can trust. The child's teacher may be the adult closest to the child outside the family. Playgroup leaders, teachers and nursery nurses will have daily contact with children and their families.

Teachers observations should make a relevant contribution to multi professional assessment and therapeutic programmes. Many documents about child abuse and training have little input from teachers (Bulter Sloss, 1988 and Stone, 1989).

Following the Cleveland Report (Butler Sloss, 1988), guidelines were issued by the DES instructing each school to appoint a senior member of staff as their named contact, who should deal with cases of suspected abuse of children in school and to cooperate with other agencies. This guidance should open the door to mutual interactions between educators and other professionals and prevent further contacts from not even beginning at the assessment stage of the process.

Educators and parental partnership

Educators have developed many strategies for parental participation, involvement and support. Daily greetings and separations are routinely managed by educators. Home visits, key person systems, regular assessment and profiling with parents and curriculum planning with parents are all features of regular conversations and consultation with children's families.

These regular and routine interactions with parents mean that confidence, trust and affection can often build up between children's families and their educators. This gives them a flying start in setting up a congruent dialogue about more delicate issues concerned with children who have been (or may have been) abused. For instance, if a teacher had been a sympathetic listener and regular source of counsel and advice, she could well seek further information about a child's bruises, her sleepiness in class, or the sexual behaviour in her play.

Enquiries from a trusted and sympathetic adult could elicit disclosures about striking a child in the fury of the moment, or allowing a child to watch videos when her parents were exhausted and stressed, or indeed of marital difficulties which could have exposed the child to violence or adult sexual activity. These disclosures might be with a class teacher or nursery nurse, made in the context of this kind of daily relationship rather than in an interview with a social worker or with health personnel. Teachers who are recipients of these kinds of confidences and disclosures must be supported and listened to by other professional colleagues. Teachers should be part of the multi-disciplinary team. They themselves need the support of social workers!

The training and experience of educators

What teachers do know about, and what about other professionals can draw on in planning work with abused children:

There are many aspects of eductors' training which are relevant to working with children who have been abused. These include:

* *Training in child development*
  Early years teachers and nursery nurses have training in child development. They will appreciate the significance of all sensory experiences and active learning situations on the child's learning.

  This understanding may support not only a teacher's curriculum plans, but also help them to promote children's learning about relationships. Their experience in this area could enable them to design and adapt other professionals therapeutic plans to enable programmes to be especially matched to how young children learn about expressing and resolving traumatic experiences.

  Part of an early years educators training and experience will be concerned with choosing play material and helping children learn vocabulary to represent grief, anger, sadness, and other emotions which abused children may need to deal with. Young children may communicate their feelings using malleable play materials rather than words. A skilled educator with the support and guidance of a play therapist may well have important work to do with children in the school, playgroup, or nursery context.

- ***Educators are experienced at talking with, and communicating to children***
  Their daily work is primarily with children, not with adults and they are often very skilled at explaining, remembering, describing, instructing and empathising with young children. This skill is even more effective when adults know something of a child's previous experiences so that they can link up a new concept to one already accommodated into a child's mind. This means teachers are ideally placed to prepare children for meetings as well as to make assessments of the child's understanding about the therapeutic process, and of possible changes in the arrangements for their care.

- ***Observation and assessment***
  Early years educators, in particular those with nursery nurse training, have substantial training in observation skills. It is important that observations of children's behaviour, or **evidence** of the summative assessments made by educators can support and illuminate multidisciplinary discussions about children. Early years educators have an important part to play because their observational evidence will be noted and informed by their knowledge of children's development. Their assessments, judgements and interpretations of these observations will depend on their values and beliefs, as well as on their knowledge of development about what is 'normal' childlike behaviour and what may be cause for concern.
  Educators often give summative assessments of children's behaviour which may be cause for concern. They use words and phrases such as 'poor concentration', 'poor speech', 'withdrawn and sad'. These assessments need to be qualified by **descriptive observational evidence** so that a multi professional therapeutic team can match the work they plan to a child's particular knowledge, skills, understanding and attitudes.

For example: 'withdrawn and sad' Observational evidence?

a) Maya wept into the nursery nurse's lap this morning. She clings to her in all group sessions and seems to draw comfort from her physical presence. She follows groups of other children into story sessions or looks on when children are discussing in a group, but does not offer her own contribution;

or

b) Maya clings on to her coat, rocks to and fro, sucks her thumb and does not appear to notice what other children are doing or saying.

I would suggest that a) might be evidence of healthy grieving. Maya is expressing her sadness and loss with a trusted adult. However b) could be evidence that her distress is overwhelming and that she would need a different kind of support to enable her to 'deal with' her feelings. In one case, 'withdrawn and sad' could be seen as a positive and healthy response to abuse and loss. The other could be seen as 'negative' and would alert professionals to her need for 'treatment'.

I use this example to consider the various interpretations that different professionals might bring to these observations and to draw attention to the fact that observational evidence, real **descriptions** of what a child does and says, are **essential** if professionals are going to make meaningful decisions about Maya's therapy. The educator has a special responsibility to contribute this information, and other professionals should be obliged to seek this kind of observational evidence.

Key training and development need for educators working in child protection

Educators may need further training in certain areas in order to make meaningful contributions to professional teams so that they can meet their obligations and responsibilities to represent the interests of children in their care. These may include:

● more training on observation, assessment and record keeping;
● more training on how our own values and beliefs formed from our own childhoods, our own cultural and ethnic backgrounds

and from our own professional training and experiences effects our interpretations, judgements and actions in relation to what we observe children doing and saying;
Both the above are addressed in the training pack '*Making Assessment Work*' (Drummond, Rouse, Pugh, 1992).

• more training on school approaches to child protection work (Evans, 1993).

• more training to introduce educators to the theory and practice of possible therapeutic options that they may need to be part of in child abuse work.

• more training on how to work to support children's emotional development.

There is a great deal of pressure on educators to create a 'happy atmosphere' with 'happy children'. This often obstructs a holistic approach to teaching children to express and accommodate a range of emotions. Educators may have the quality of their provision judged on this criteria. Observers expect to see obedient, compliant, cooperative, smiling and even tempered 'happy' children. This may cut across their curriculum objective of meeting the emotional needs of children and the paramountcy of a child centred curriculum as opposed to a curriculum in response to parents and governors/managers expectations;

• more training to help teachers and other educators to confront their own emotions.

The more we learn about children's experience of abuse and our responsibilities to protect them and support them, the greater is the need for educators for comfort and supervision to address their own emotions and responses to the children they may be working with. Equally important is for educators who may have been abused themselves to have support so that they can analyse their own responses to children and think about what is acceptable and not acceptable in respect of their observations of children's play and talk. A system of supervision and support from line managers must facilitate this process;

• more opportunities to explore what is 'normal' child sexuality and curiosity and what is inappropriate sexual behaviour of children in the context of society today. This may be incongruent with educators own childhood experiences;

- more training to help educators develop anti-discriminatory practice. A more rigorous approach to considering the child's ethnicity and culture, gender and disability and the impact this has on observation and assessment. It is important to examine our own perspective and that of others. Educators should refrain from making assumptions or using stereotypes about children or their families;

- more time to think about multi-professional partnership which is based on the child's needs being paramount. Educators must take time to explore confidentiality in relation to child protection issues. This must not be confused with keeping confidences or colluding with parents because it maybe uncomfortable or because of being fearful of jeopardising the relationship. Educators must not allow the adult's needs to overwhelm or overshadow the needs of the child;

- more opportunities for inter-agency work which will create positive professional networks and opportunities to breakdown professional isolation, share information about roles and promote communication where there is no crisis. Educators need to be a focus for advocating for the needs, voice/view of the child.

The last three points are illustrated diagrammatically in Figure 5.1.

Figure 5.1 Child development, child protection, observation and assessment, the Children Act 1989

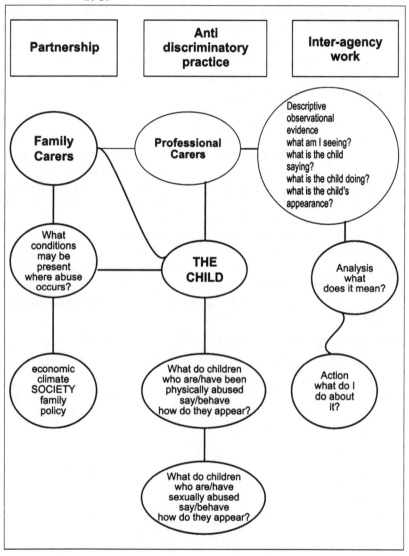

Activity

During the workshop, participants took part in the following activity:

Observations and assessments of children who have been or may have been abused must include descriptive evidence.

Descriptive evidence supports professionals in making sensitive interpretations and tentative judgements.

These judgements will inform therapeutic plans.

Aim

To give the workshop participants practice in differentiating summative assessments from descriptive observational evidence and practice in writing observational evidence.

We are looking to support those working directly with children to make descriptive observations that will inform assessments of a child's development where there are child protection concerns as well as descriptive observational evidence that may indicate abuse and the effects of abuse in young children. Observations can also indicate where the child may be helped to work through their difficulties.

Small group tasks

1. Choose two or three observations from the notes below and discuss and note down possible interpretations.
2. Make up descriptive observational evidence for:
   'whingey and upset' or 'lethargic', or 'boisterous and exuberant'.

The following are *observations made by nursery workers* in the day nursery.

At nine months Julie started attending day nursery on her own.

On her first day she settled straight into the routine, playing pleasantly all day. She needed staff to feed her. Julie can sit unaided but made no attempt to move. When laid on her stomach she tried to shuffle backwards.

24.4.89   *Julie presents as clean, tidy, responding well to Mum, reaching up for her when she appears, beginning to crawl, pleasant and happy, shows emotion appropriately, intellectually meeting her milestone.*

16.6.89   *Julie very dirty, especially feet and knees, inappropriately clothed for hot day, very floppy in movements and wobbly when held on her legs.*

4.8.89   *Julie getting upset this morning, screwing up her face and starting to cry when being spoken to, strong smell of urine on her vest which was quite stained and she had a sore bottom.*

10.89   *Julie is quiet, blends into the background but smiles when staff talk to her. Meeting milestones but at a slower rate.*

24.7.90   *Development satisfactory and no particular areas of concern. Julie usual happy self and displays not signs of distress or disturbance. Mum's explanation for bruising accepted as plausible given lack of other indicators.*

12.10.90   *When member of staff scratching her ear caused Julie to flinch at upraised hand and flinched each time the staff member did this.*

11.6.91   *Happy enough at centre, could be subdued and prone to crying for no apparent reason.*

6.8.91   *Julie has started to stand alone and cry, no tears, she just puts her hands to her face and makes a whining noise, then paces backwards and forwards waiting for staff to notice her. Once she has been given a cuddle (she still doesn't relax when held) she will go and play again.*

Observations made by nursery school teacher

Julie started school age three and a half.

She settled into nursery environment immediately and wasn't tearful at separation.

Julie presents well grown, cheerful, happy go lucky, clean and appropriately dressed (usually trousers and a jumper) for nursery activities. She enjoys boisterous games. She particularly likes to play with one boy.

Julie does not seek adult attention or chat with nursery staff, they never hear anything of Julie's home life.

Julie does not always readily respond to instructions from adults. She does not appear over disciplined. She is never sulky or cowed. She was observed crying only once.

Julie is very exuberant when playing on outdoor equipment at nursery and often takes tumbles.

'Julie didn't look like an abused child'.

References

Butler Sloss, E (1988) *Report of the Enquiry into Child Abuse in Cleveland in 1987.* HMSO

David, T (1993) *Child Protection and Early Years Teachers, Coping with Child Abuse.* Open University Press

Department of Health and Social Security (1988) *Protecting Children – A Guide for Social Workers Undertaking a Comprehensive Assessment.* HMSO

Drummond, MJ, Rouse, D, Pugh, G (1992) *Making Assessment Work, Values and Principles in assessing young children's learning.* NES/Arnold and National Children's Bureau

Evans, G (1993) *Child Protection a Whole Curriculum Approach.* Avec Designs Ltd

Gilkes, J (1989) 'Coming to Terms with Sexual Abuse: a day care perspective', *in* Riches, P. (ed) *Responses to Cleveland: improving Services for child sexual abuse.* Children & Society Special Publication: National Children's Bureau

Home Office and others (1991) *Working Together, Under the Children Act 1989. A Guide to arrangements for inter-agency co-operation for the protection of children from abuse.* HMSO

Kitzinger, J (1990) 'Who Are You Kidding? Children, Power, and the Struggle Against Sexual Abuse', *in* James, A and Prout, A *Constructing and Reconstructing Childhood.* Falmer Press

Lahad, M (1992) 'Story-Making in Assessment method for coping with stress, six-piece story-making and BASIC Ph' *in* Jennings, S. *Dramatherapy.* Tavistock-Routeledge Press

Pen Green Family Centre (1990) *Learning to be Strong: developing assertiveness in young children.* Changing Perspectives Ltd

Phillips, M., and Dutt, R (1991) *Towards a Black Perspective in Child Protection.* Race Equality Unit, National Institute of Social Work

Stone, F (ed) (1989) *Child Abuse: The Scottish Experience.* BAAF

Wattam, C (1990) *Teacher's Experiences with Children Who Have or May Have Been Sexually Abused.* NSPCC

First hand accounts of child abuse from survivors of abuse

Allison, D (1993) *Bastard out of Carolina*. Flamingo original
Angelou, M (1984) *I Know Why the Caged Bird Sings*. Virago
Attwood, M (1989) *Cat's Eye*. Bloomsbury
Rouf, K 'My self in echoes. My voice in song' *in* Bannister, A,
    Barrett, K, Shearer, E (Ed) (1990) *Listening to Children, the Pro-
    fessional Response to Hearing the Abused Child*. Longman
Spring, J (1987) *Cry Hard and Swim: The story of an incest survivor*.
    Virago

6. Managing therapeutic work in a family centre

Bridie Speller
Project Manager
Stevenage Family Centre

Based on my experience at Stevenage Family Centre. I have focused on some of the conflicts which occur in providing a range of services from one small integrated centre. These are identified in the dilemmas between:

- 'community' work and 'referred' work; and
- therapeutic work and child protection.

I hope to enable members of the workshop to examine these and consider the implications for practice through brainstorming and case study exercises.

Stevenage Family Centre is run by the National Children's Home in partnership with Hertfordshire Social Services. It was set up six years ago and now has a staff team of seven (mostly part-time), supported by a secretary, a domestic worker and a driver. Based in an ordinary three-bedroomed semi-detached house on an estate at the southern end of town, its services are limited by its size but have developed since 1987 through increased initiatives in community work and use of volunteers and sessional workers. The staff have a variety of qualifications including CQSW, NNEB, Youth and Community Diploma, Counselling. There is an emphasis on partnership with other professionals and recognition that families often need more specialist help than can be provided within the Centre.

The work of the Centre can be divided into three main areas:

- centre-based services;
- family support scheme;
- preventive work.

More details are given in the Appendix to this chapter.

The overall aims are to provide a range of services to families with children under ten where there is a perceived need or where those children are considered to be 'at risk'. The centre aims to enable families to make changes which will enhance their functioning and improve the quality of the lives of individuals within the family.

To meet these aims, the range of services can be seen as a menu from which choices can be made to suit the different needs of both families and individuals. The model which has evolved is similar to that described as 'integrated' or 'family resource centres' (Phelan, 1983; Warren, 1986; Gill, 1988). Whilst the centre originally worked with a small number of 'referred families', it is now able to reach many more families experiencing either short term, minor difficulties or more serious difficulties and where there are clear issues over the safety and protection of the children. The needs of each family can be met at various levels at different times, and regular reviews can enable referring agencies and families to reassess priorities and needs and match these with appropriate resources.

The literature on development of family centres tends to equate the 'referred' centres with therapeutic work, where much emphasis is placed on work with individuals or families, and the workers' skills will be in areas such as family therapy, psychotherapy or psychoanalysis. At the other end of the spectrum a 'community' model places emphasis on neighbourhood base where staff have skills in bringing families and groups together and enabling them to participate and to empower them in an effort to overcome common difficulties and stresses.

There are some inevitable conflicts when these diverse aims are brought together. Will the centre become a 'jack of all trades' – master of none? The expectations of the various users of the centre may be different, and local people may be wary of using services which seem designed for 'problem' families, whilst community resources dominated by more articulate and assertive individuals may exclude families in real need of help. However, the advantages are also considerable. There is a very real 'destigmatisation' of the centre and the work when there is a wide variety of users, and there is more likely to be a good matching of needs to resources where the services are more varied. There can be a greater encouragement of participation and progression towards personal and group change can be facilitated.

A continuum of the services could be seen thus:

Community	Preventive/supportive	Therapeutic	Protective
education	befriending	support	monitoring
recreation	supportive	treatment	checking
self-	mutual	healing	assessment
development	volunteer-		intervention
empowerment	client or		
	worker		
	group		

Families and individuals may be referred or refer themselves to any point on the continuum, but with careful assessment at referral and at reviews they may be helped best by use of a variety of services at once, or at different times. Changes in circumstances and priorities can be dealt with more easily.

Stress factors leading to poor parenting or abuse will vary in number and priority and may therefore be addressed at different levels. I would maintain that a 'package' of services can be seen as therapeutic overall, in that it aims to relieve those stresses and improve family and individual functioning.

The issues for management of the work in an integrated centre are obviously complex. As suggested, there is some inevitable conflict between community work and therapeutic work, similarly, therapeutic work with families does not always fit easily with child protection especially in respect of clients' expectations. These conflicts need to be recognised and addressed at every stage in order to counteract confusions. A commitment to partnership with both parents and other agencies, as envisaged in the Children Act, requires honesty and openness. Margolin says 'it is the therapists ethical responsibility to abdicate the role of relationship adviser and help a threatened person find protection'; it must be clear that in every situation, family centre workers must and will put the child's safety and interests first, and whilst information shared is treated confidentially, when this indicates a threat to a child the worker's duty is to protect the child. This applies at all levels of the service, including community groups, playschemes and so on and needs to be understood by staff, volunteers and users alike. If there is also discussion with parents prior to the passing on of such information a trusting relationship with the family is more likely to be maintained.

The 'package' offered to families referred to Stevenage Family Centre is based on information given in the referral form; emphasis is placed on the need for the family to be fully involved in this process, and services offered should fulfil the needs perceived by the families themselves, and even when a family is referred as part of a requirement from a child protection case conference, there should be some common understanding of needs between the family and workers. A mother may accept that she and her children could benefit from time away from cramped, poor housing and an offer of support based on this will lay the foundations for more sophisticated therapy later. A monthly meeting – called a 'family meeting' to emphasise the family's role in it – brings together family members, key worker, and other professionals if necessary, to assess progress based on the initial contract. Observations from recording at the centre may be used to focus on new areas to develop and new goals can be set. Some of these should always be short-term and achievable (for example, to keep to an agreed bedtime routine for a child or to visit a child's school to talk to his teacher). At these meetings, referral can be made to other groups or services within the centre, or a decision made to approach other agencies for help (no staff team can provide all the skills needed to deal with complex family difficulties plus the individual needs of each family member!)

Stevenage has no other family centre or similar resource, so the small team have developed some ways of meeting the demands produced by a population of 78,000. Referred families have a time-limited contract with a maximum of one year at the centre, the average stay is eight months. The support can be extended by use of volunteer 'befrienders' and referral on to groups run by the 'preventive' workers or other community resources. This helps to focus the therapeutic input and to set priorities. The aim is always to enable a family to find new support systems for themselves whilst developing their potential to do so through the work done at the centre. Communication between the workers involved in each of the areas of service is a constant agenda in order to maximise use of resources.

Finally, the process of providing therapeutic services does not stand still and evaluation is essential to good practice. Feedback from both users and referral agencies is now built in to the work with each referred family and group.

References

Gill, O (1988) 'Integrated work in neighbourhood family centres', *Practice*, 2,3, 243-255

Phelan, J (1983) *Family Centres: a study*. Children's Society

Warren, C (1986) 'Towards a family centre movement: reconciling day care, child protection and community work', *Child Abuse Review*, 1,3, 10-16

Appendix 6.1

Stevenage Family Centre Services

Centre-based services
Women's Group
Survivors Group
Young Parents
Family Sessions 0-5s
Family Sessions 5-10s
Family Sessions 0-10s
Parents Support Group
Fathers' Group
Contact Visits
Joint Work with other Professionals
Home Visits

Family Support Scheme
Parent-to-Parent Support
1)   Sessional Workers
2)   Volunteers
Crisis/Emergency Support
Home-Based Support
Activity-Based Support

Preventive Work (Two part-time social workers)
Support for existing community groups
Initiatives to develop new resources
Research and liaison to establish needs and gaps in provision for children under 10
Individual work with children-sessional workers
Parenting groups in community
'Drop-in'
After-school care
Summer holiday playscheme for children 'at risk'

Emphasis on groups being or becoming consumer run

Appendix 6.2

Stevenage family centre

Centre based services timetable

Time	Monday	Tuesday	Wednesday	Thursday	Friday
9.00				Referrals and Allocation Meeting	
9.30			Families with under-fives / Focus on child development and assessment		
10.00	Women's Group / Creche / Health / Assetiveness / Self-esteem	Young Prents / Parenting / Health / Education		Centre available for contact visits, individual or family work	Family Day / (Primarily for under 5s) / Parenting skills / Assessment / Counselling / Home-making skills / Social skills / Budgeting
12.00					
12.30		Staff lunch			
1.00				Parents Support Group / Creche Parenting / Mutual Support	
1.30	Survivors Group / For women who have been abused	Staff meeting			
2.00		Centre available for contact visits, individual or family work	Families with five to ten year-olds / Discussion group (parenting)		
3.00	Centre available for contact visits, individual or family work			Contact visits	Contact visits, etc
3.15 – 3.45			School 'Pick up' / Family time		
6.00					
7.00	Family Support Scheme / Sessional workers meeting (fortnightly)	Family Support Scheme / Volunteers meeting (fortnightly) / Volunteer induction and training	Fathers' Group	Survivors group 2 (Self-support group)	
9.00					

7. Selecting, training and supporting volunteers to work with vulnerable families

Ann Pemberton, Senior Organiser
Leeds Home-Start

Home-Start is a voluntary organisation which uses volunteers to visit families in their own homes during a period of stress or difficulty. The volunteers offer caring support and befriending on a flexible basis for as long as the family need this support.

Leeds Home-Start is affiliated to the Home-Start Consultancy in Leicester and therefore operates to the same standards and methods of practice as all other Home-Start schemes both nationally and internationally, but as with all other schemes we are funded and managed locally and are therefore quite autonomous.

Much of the success of Home-Start lies in the commitment of its volunteers and the 'professionalism' of its paid organisers in each scheme, whose responsibility it is to recruit, prepare and support the scheme's volunteers.

Leeds Home-Start currently have 56 volunteers who have attended a preparation course for one day a week for 10 weeks and are then supported by the paid organisers.

Many of the families supported by Leeds Home-Start would be considered to be 'vulnerable families'.

The Workshop aimed to enable participants to:

- acknowledge that there is a role for volunteers and have an understanding of that role;
- identify good practice in recruitment, training, and support of volunteers by having an overview of Leeds Home-Start practice in these fields.

It aimed to do this by:

- defining the term 'vulnerable families' (dictionary definition of vulnerable – 'that may be wounded, susceptible of injury, exposed to damage by weapon, criticism and so on');
- identifying what 'damaged' families are 'vulnerable' to – internal and external;
- looking at what effect this 'damage' has on families;
- acknowledging that the presence of a number of these factors at any one time could indicate the possibility of a child protection issue arising in the family;

- using a case study to identify what the role of the volunteer might be in a 'vulnerable family':

  — what the referrer might want the volunteer to do?
  — what might the family want/need?
  — what could the volunteer offer?

- examining what worries statutory workers about using volunteers;
- looking at how we recruit, train and support *suitable* volunteers.

Recruitment

The participants looked closely at Leeds Home-Start practice.

Leeds Home-start recruitment procedure

Advertising

Adverts are placed in the local free press asking people who may be interested to phone in.

Leaflets with the advert on are distributed through a number of organisations' newsletters such as:

- PPA
- Equal Opportunities Unit, Leeds City Council

Posters are displayed in a variety of public places:

- Health centres
- Community centres
- Adult education centres

- Doctors' surgeries
- Womens' centres
- nurseries

On receipt of a phone call prospective volunteers are asked interview with one of the organisers.

The first interview

Leeds Home-Start interview prospective volunteers for the first time in the office, but make every effort to create a relaxed atmosphere.

The organisers will outline the scheme and what is expected from its volunteers and will encourage the prospective volunteer to talk about themselves and their own abilities. The organisers will ask questions which will reveal some of the prospective volunteer's attitudes.

The organisers will answer any questions that the prospective volunteers may have.

At the end of this interview prospective volunteers are asked to take away a 'volunteer's application form' and give some more thought to the scheme. If they wish to pursue it further, to return the form completed and an organiser will contact them to arrange a home visit. The application form also requires **two character references.**

The second interview

This interview gives the prospective volunteer an opportunity to ask any further questions.

The organiser will ask the prospective volunteer to talk about the skills and abilities they are able to bring to Home-Start.

References

All references are taken up.

Preparation Course

At the end of this interview process prospective volunteers are asked to join our course of preparation.

Most organisers feel that they will know whether their volunteers are suited to Home-Start after they have completed the course of preparation, and it is the organisers' final decision whether or not to introduce a volunteer to a family.

When selecting potential volunteers, organisers try to avoid those who say they never had any problems and those who seem to have had far too many.

Preparation (Training)

Participants looked at Leeds Home-Start ten week course of preparation for volunteers; at the volunteers' role in preventative work and child protection; and identified the need for on-going training and external inter-agency training.

Leeds Home-start Preparation Course 1993

3 March 1993
am   Getting to Know! Home-Start video.
pm   Fear and Anxieties.
        What I Want From This Course.

10 March 1993
am   Home-Start Nationally and Locally.
        Standards and Methods of Practice.
        Insurance.
pm   Role of the Volunteer.

17 March 1993
am   Commitment – Margaret Scally (Vice Chairperson).
pm   Ethics of Home Visiting.

24 March 1993
am   Meeting Working Volunteers.
pm   Confidentiality.

31 March 1993
am   Support and Supervision.
pm   Child Protection – Frances Mawston.

Easter Break

21 April 1993
am   Listening Skills – Womens' Counselling and Therapy.
pm   What is a Family?

28 April 1993
am   HIV/AIDS – Karen Wallis.
pm   Domestic Violence – Speaker.

5 May 1993
am   Equal Opportunities – Attitudes or Prejudices.

pm   Children and the Law – Stephanie Martins.

12 May 1993

am   Visiting Families of Different Ethnic Groups -
        Beryl Juma/Sanjay.

pm   Administration/Insurance Cover.

19 May 1993

am   Loss and Ending.

pm   Evaluation – Dorothy Brown (Chair: Management
        Committee).

Support

Participants explored why it is *essential* that volunteers have access
to paid workers for whom supporting volunteers is a key part of
their role, and identified that support has to be a common thread
throughout the organisation. It has to be someone's responsibility.
There is a clear procedure for accessibility.

- Volunteers *must* understand its importance.
- volunteers *must* be encouraged to use it appropriately.

Supporting volunteers

- ***Between volunteers and Leeds Home-Start organiser***
  This form of support is essential. Volunteers should feel that
  they can talk freely with the organisers about their visits to their
  families, and about their own personal problems if necessary.
      Leeds Home-Start organisers are available to visit the volun-
  teers at home or accompany them on a joint visit to the family.
      Volunteers have one morning a week when they know that
  the organisers will definitely be available in the office for either
  face to face support or to talk to on the phone. Group support
  meetings are arranged for volunteers.
- ***Between volunteer and volunteer***
  The volunteers will have an opportunity of getting to know one
  another during the course of preparation and of meeting more
  experienced volunteers, so they are able to offer one another
  individual support as necessary in the course of their work.
- ***Volunteers and on-going training***
  On-going training sessions are arranged at which speakers from

relevant professions are invited to cover topics of common interest.

• *Informal support*

Volunteers welcome the opportunity of participating in social events and activities throughout the year. Volunteers receive a regular monthly bulletin containing information about the scheme's activities.

Volunteers find it useful to have a list of the names and addresses and phone numbers of all the volunteers in the scheme.

The payment of volunteers' expenses is an extremely important form of support.

Conclusion

What gives referring agencies confidence in using volunteers to work with 'vulnerable families'.

Good practice in:

• recruitment;
• preparation (training);
• support.

8. A multidisciplinary approach to child protection

Louise Humphries
Royal Southants Hospital

This workshop was centred on the Department of Health publication **Working Together,** the aim of which was to establish why we need to work together and if this is in fact happening in practice.

Delegates represented a wide cross section of professionals including health, social services, voluntary services and education. All delegates worked either directly or closely allied to the field of child protection as trainers, managers, field workers and councillors.

The group was positive about their experiences to date and their hopes for the future. There were however many areas of difficulties and concerns which were identified. The overriding issue from the group was the concern at the current lack of resources which many departments are facing. This was represented in a number of ways: from the lack of funding for attending educational courses, to the freezing of posts causing the remaining staff to increase their caseloads with the inevitable rise in stress levels (always present in this highly stressful area of work). The trainers in the group felt that they were at times being expected to train in a climate of resistance due to the demands felt by fieldwork staff of actually doing the job.

Those delegates representing the voluntary sector expressed feelings of being left out at times and on occasion not being considered or consulted to the level that they would wish and their contribution sometimes seeming to be left unheeded.

The group as a whole were very positive at the increasing openness and focus of working with parent/carers in relation to enabling the parent/carers to protect their child. They did however clearly identify that at times partnership with parent/carers and protecting the child may represent a conflict of interest with the need to focus on the child being paramount. Generally the group felt that this was not well recognised at a more senior level.

Many in the group whose jobs involved crossing professional disciplines described their experience of apparent resistance at more senior management level to the need for openness and the sharing of information and ideas.

The majority of the group identified the need for a greater participation of medicine in this field, ranging from the lack of representation at case conferences to the reluctance of providing written information in relation to the child. Concern was generally expressed at the difficulty many of the delegates have experienced when attempting to work with some of those in the medical profession.

9. A community approach to child protection

Joan Lister, Headteacher
Ashfield Nursery School
Jan Rogers, Headteacher
Cruddas Park Nursery School
Newcastle-upon-Tyne

The workshop concentrated on identifying what is meant by community and how a multidisciplinary approach to child protection work within the community can be developed.

The group trialled one of the modules from **Protection through Prevention** (Bartlett 1991) – a training pack developed by our two nursery schools and the child protection coordinator for Newcastle.

The **Protection through Prevention** materials were designed to support group leaders to achieve the following:

- to raise awareness about the signs, symptoms and circumstances which may indicate child abuse and child sexual abuse;
- to raise awareness and develop understanding of national and local procedures and guidelines;
- to provide opportunities for course participants to examine their own (and other people's) beliefs, values and prejudices in order to improve their ability to listen, communicate and interpret information;
- to provide opportunities for course participants to examine their own (and other people's) approaches to defining and solving problems in order to develop preventative strategies;
- to provide opportunities for course participants to improve

their ability to communicate in one-to-one and small group interactions;

- to provide opportunities for course participants to improve their ability to communicate in large group interactions;
- to provide opportunities for course participants to clarify their personal and/or professional development priorities in relation to child protection work;
- to encourage the development of professional and community networks which contribute positively to the protection of children;
- to create a basis for engaging the child, family and community in a **Protection through Prevention** programme, in the spirit of the 1989 Children Act.

The materials are flexible enough to allow group leaders to include other aims, taking account of the local context and the composition of the groups with whom they are working. The course is modular, and each of the nine modules has detailed guidance for group leaders, as well as photocopiable materials for participants.

These course materials have been designed to be especially useful to groups who are developing interdisciplinary approaches to child protection, working within the spirit of the Children Act. **Protection through Prevention** assumes that there is a great deal that we can all do, as professionals and as members of the community, to protect children from abuse, by the active development of preventative strategies.

The modular design is flexible enough to yield to a variety of inservice education requirements. For instance, the first three modules can be used alone, as foundation training, by local authorities or by non-governmental organisations who wish to raise the awareness of large numbers of people. The whole programme, which lasts about thirty hours, can also be used as a five-day block course, or as a course extended over several weeks or months.

The materials are based on the work of a team of Newcastle child protection workers. Their approach is family centred, recognising the significant role that can be played by parents and the community in protecting children's rights to safety. The materials are the outcome of collaboration between individuals, professional groups and institutions, from health, education and the social services and emphasise the importance of developing close collaborative links between the various agencies who might be involved in child protection.

The course has been carefully constructed to help group leaders to create a supportive learning environment for their course members, where it will be safe for course members to express their personal concerns about confronting difficult child abuse issues, working with people from other disciplines, or working with parents and the community.

In the introduction to the pack, Brian Roycroft, Director of Social Services, City of Newcastle-upon-Tyne wrote:

> 'This training programme provides a comprehensive range of training materials. Developed from a partnership between social services and education, it provides a high quality interdisciplinary training programme for child protection.
> **Protection through Prevention** fully meets the spirit, values and philosophy expounded in the 1989 Children Act and the 1991 **Working Together** guidelines and I strongly recommend **Protection through Prevention** to those involved in child protection training and staff development. In my judgement, it represents a unique, well conceived and flexibly designed staff development programme for use in interdisciplinary child protection training'.

The module chosen for the workshop **Personal Beliefs** enabled the group to work in pairs and foursomes to identify the advantages and disadvantages of working in the community. The group placed a great deal of importance on concentrating not only personal beliefs and worth but also on recognising the value of others' roles and valuing everyone's contribution to child protection – professionals, volunteers and parents.

The group also explored other publications linked with child protection – **Learning to be Strong** (Pen Green, 1990) and Kidscape's (1988) **Under Five's Programme** – as well as looking at the whole **Protection through Prevention** package.

Details of these packs are given in the **Bibliography**.

10. Bibliography

Prepared by Ann Robinson and Gillian Potkins,
Early Childhood Unit, National Children's Bureau.

Child Protection: working with young children

Adams, J and Llewellyn, A (1991) 'A puppet video to prevent sexual abuse in young children'. *Association for Child Psychology, and Psychiatry Newsletter*, 13, 1, 15-22
Describes an evaluation of a video aimed at teaching 3-7 year olds to recognise sexually abusive touching, and how to protect themselves.
Adcock, M, White, R and Hollows, A. (1991) *'Child Protection. A training and practice resource pack for work under the Children Act 1989'.* Trainers and Participants' packs. National Children's Bureau. Papers and Course Notes 85 pages, Resources and Glossary 55 pages.
For social work or law practitioners who make decisions about children at risk, but also useful for others such as guardians ad litem.
Bartlett, R (Ed) (1991) *'Protection through Prevention: Child protection, a programme for interdisciplinary staff development'.* Changing Perspectives Ltd, The Verdin Exchange, High Street, Winsford, Cheshire. 90 pages, plus 9 modules, in folder.
A complete 30-hour course for use with single-discipline or multidisciplinary groups.
Bellman, M and others (1991) *Keeping Children Healthy. A guide for under fives workers.* Starting Points, no. 8. (Edited by C. Zealey). VOLCUF, 77 Holloway Road, London N7 8JZ. 23 pages.
Includes a section on recognising and dealing with child abuse.
Berrick, JD. (1991) 'Sexual abuse prevention training for pre-

schoolers: Implications for moral development', *Children and Youth Services Review*, 13, 1/2, 61-75

Bookman, S (1990) 'Never too young to learn', *Mother and Baby*, October, pages 66-68.
Encourages parents to teach children to protect themselves from the danger of abuse from strangers, or from someone he or she knows.

California Child Care Resource and Referral Network (1989) *Making a difference. A handbook for child care providers.* With booklet for parents: 'Choosing Child Care'. 2nd edition. San Francisco, California: 809 Lincoln Way, SF, CA 94122, USA. 72 pages.
Distributed to all day nurseries and child carers in the state. Guidelines on administration. Sections on working with children, observing children in daycare, multicultural care. Mainly concerns issues of identifying and dealing with possible physical, emotional or sexual abuse in young children.

Campion, J. (1992) *Working with Vulnerable Young Children.* Cassell.

Cohn, DS (1991) 'Anatomical doll play of preschoolers referred for sexual abuse and those not referred', *Child Abuse and Neglect*, 15, 4, 455-466

David, T (1991) 'Child abuse', *Child Education*, 68, 4, 21
Looks at issues facing teachers in coming to terms with cases of child abuse, and at the lack of appropriate training and materials.

David, T (1993) *'Child Protection and Early Years Teachers. Coping with child abuse'.* Open University Press. 166 pages.
Suggests the roles that teachers and nursery nurses can take in identifying abused children, and in helping them and their families. Examines the cultural and historical background of child abuse and neglect.

Dean, C (1991) 'Armed with strong words in steel town'. *Times Educational Supplement*, 7/6/1991, page 14.
The "Learning to be Strong" assertiveness training programme at Pen Green Family Centre in Corby helps four-year-olds deal with bullies, and other unwanted attentions.
See also: Pen Green *and* Walters

Elliott, M (1986) *'Keeping Safe. A practical guide to talking with children'.* Bedford Square Press/NCVO. 72 pages.
Step by step guide to help parents and others to talk with children about potentially dangerous situations, and ways of dealing with them.

Entwistle, I and Bryan, B (1992) *'Health Education in the Early Years'*. British Association for Early Childhood Education. 16 pages.
Includes a section on My World: Keeping safe in my neighbourhood.
Evans, G *'Child Protection. A whole curriculum approach'*.
AVEC Designs Ltd, PO Box 709, Bristol BS99 1GE (Tel: 0272 241 380).
Materials developed over 5 years in primary and special schools in Avon. Teaching resources and INSET resources, including video.
Family Rights Group and National Society For The Prevention Of Cruelty To Children (1992) *Child Protection Procedures – what they mean for your family*. NSPCC/FRG. 83 pages.
Aimed at families who find themselves involved in child protection procedures. Incorporates changes under the Children Act.
Gilkes, J (1988) 'Coming to terms with sexual abuse: A day care perspective', *Children & Society*, 2, 3, 261-269
Describes how a group of nursery workers attempt to come to terms with identifying abuse, understanding their own feelings, and integrating a preventive approach into the nursery curriculum.
Gillham, B (1989) *Play Safe. Never go with a stranger*. Little Mammoth, Mandarin Paperbacks. (Reissue, originally 1988). Unpaginated.
Bright illustrations and simple text make this book accessible to young children, telling them how to cope with approaches from strangers.
Greater Manchester And Lancashire Implementation Strategy Group (1990)
'Building in the race and culture dimensions into implementation strategies'.
Paper 1: Prevention and support services, including day care services and services for children in need.
Paper 2: Child protection issues and legal orders.
Bury Social Services Department (Children Act 1989: Focus Group on Race and Culture). Two papers, each of 2 pages.
Two sets of questions that those providing or registering day care facilities should be asking.
Hallett, C and Birchall, E (1992), *Coordination and Child Protection: A review of the literature*. Department of Sociology and Social Policy, University of Stirling. HMSO. 373 pages.
Haskett, ME and Kistner, JA (1991), Social interactions and peer

perceptions of young physically abused children. *Child Development*, 62, 5, 979-990
Comparison with non-abused children in a day care facility.
Hewitt, SK (1991), 'Therapeutic management of preschool cases of alleged but unsubstantiated sexual abuse', *Child Welfare (US)*, 70, 1, 59-67
Hollwey, S (1991), Recognising child sexual abuse. *Montessori Courier*, vol. 2, no. 6, pages 18-19.
Using a case history, describes the symptoms that teachers and those caring for young children should be aware of, and what they should do.
Home Office, and others (1991), *Working Together Under the Children Act 1989: A guide to arrangements for inter-agency co-operation for the protection of children from abuse.* HMSO. 126 pages.
Kidscape (1988), *Under Five's Programme. For planning and teaching good sense defence to children.*
Kidscape Ltd, 82 Brook Street, London W1Y 1YG. 52 pages.
A manual for all those working in education with under fives, to be used with parts 1,2 & 3 of the Kidscape Primary Kit, and replacing part 4.
Kitzinger, J (1990), 'Who are you kidding? Children, power, and the struggle against sexual abuse', *in* James, A and Prout, A *Constructing and Reconstructing Childhood.* Falmer Press. Pages 157-183.
Argues that abuse is not an anomaly but part of the structural oppression of children in our society and this must be addressed rather than attempting to empower or protect children.
McMahon, L (1992), *The Handbook of Play Therapy.* Tavistock/Routledge. 237 pages.
Includes chapters on working with disability, bereavement, divorce, sexual abuse and children in care.
Pen Green Family Centre (1990), *Learning To Be Strong: Developing assertiveness with young children.*
Changing Perspectives Ltd, The Verdin Exchange, High Street, Winsford, Cheshire. 39 pages.
Materials developed at Pen Green, aimed at helping young children 'learn to be strong' at school and outside school, preparing them to deal with strangers, and to deal with different kinds of abuse. Includes bibliographies of supporting books for children and adults, and evaluations and reviews of the development sessions.
Richman, N and others (1988), 'Child abuse', *in* Richman, N *and*

Lansdown, R (Eds) *Problems of Preschool Children*. John Wiley and Sons. Pages 97-110.
Types of abuse; recognising abuse; causes of abuse; sexual abuse; helping the child; working with the family; outcomes.
Ruxton, S (1992), 'What's HE doing at the family centre?', *The Dilemmas of Men who Care for Children*.
National Children's Home, 85 Highbury Park, N5 1UD. 59 pages.
Perspectives on men in child care. Gender roles and welfare. A survey of NCH Family Centres, including the questionnaire.
Sivan, AB (1991), 'Preschool child development: Implications for investigation of child abuse allegations', *Child Abuse and Neglect*, 15, 4, 485-493
Reviews research and theories of pre-school child development and their relevance to the debate over veracity of allegations.
Sloane, R (1991), 'Cooperating with the police', *Nursery World*, 91, 3262, 16-17
In Cambridgeshire community police men and women regularly visit playgroups to talk about matters such as road safety and talking to strangers.
Tissier, G and others (1991), 'A world of good intentions', *Community Care*, 884, 11-14
Variety of perspectives on the Children Act covering: care proceedings; guardians ad litem; child protection; disabled children; under eights.
Wakefield Joint Child Protection Committee (1992?) *Inter Agency Child Protection*. Handbook of Practices and Procedures.
Wakefield Social Services Department. 158 pages.
Detailed handbook covering policy, legal framework including the 1989 Children Act, child protection register, abuse recognition and investigation, protection and planning, assessment and review, agency procedures, allegations against carers or staff, document formats.
Walters, T (1991), 'Learning to be strong', *Nursery World*, 91, 3285, 12-13
Children at Pen Green Family Centre in Corby are practising assertiveness training and learning to be strong.
Webb, S (1991). 'Safe kids', *Social Work Today*, 22, 37, 18-19
Describes a Leeds group project to help small children come to terms with sexual abuse.
Webster, A (1993), 'Child protection – a whole curriculum', *Child Education*, 70, 1, 42-43

Describes a programme in Avon, developed by Gill Evans, which sets out to meet the needs of all children, and to encourage them to positively protect themselves.

Woolfson, R (1992), 'Why so shy?', *Nursery World,* 92, 3301,18-19
Shyness can affect all children, but when a previously gregarious child suddenly becomes shy, nursery workers should consider the possibility of a more serious problem.

Wurtele, SK and Schmitt, A (1992), 'Child care workers' knowledge about reporting suspected child sexual abuse', *Child Abuse and Neglect,* 16, 3, 385-390

Wurtele, SK (1992), 'A comparison of teachers versus parents as instructors of a personal safety program for preschoolers'. *Child Abuse and Neglect,* 16, 1, 127-137

Wurtele, SK, Kast, LC and Melzer, AM (1992), 'Sexual abuse prevention education for young children: A comparison of teachers and parents as instructors', *Child Abuse and Neglect,* 16, 6, 865-876
Sample used was made up of 172 HeadStart preschoolers.

Zero To Three/national Center For Clinical Infant Programs: Violence Study Group (1993)
Call for violence prevention and intervention on behalf of the very young children.

USA: Zero to Three, 2000 14th St N, Arlington VA 22201. 6 pages and 4 pages press release.
The Study Group is promoting a three point agenda: family-centered approaches to addressing trauma/prevention; a realignment of values; informed comprehensive public policy strategies for reducing violence.

Index

see also doctors; early years; health;
  multidisciplinary; nurseries;
  police; psychologists; social
  workers; teachers
prosecutions, success rate 18, 27
protection *see* child protection
Protection through Prevention 88-90
psychiatric disorders 15
  see also behavioural
psychiatric services 26
  see also counselling; doctors; health
  professionals; therapy
psychological adjustment
  mechanisms of abused
  children 11-12
psychological ill-treatment 8, 22-3
psychologists 19, 26, 46
  see also health professionals; therapy

R
recruitment of volunteers 81-3
referral *see* reporting abuse
regulations for day care 46-8
reporting abuse 19, 59
reviewing procedure 76
rights *see* children's rights; parents'
  rights
Rogers, Jan 88-90
Rouse, Dorothy 58-70
Royal College of Physicians 18-19
Royal Southants Hospital 86

S
St. James' Hospital, Leeds 7
scalds 14
sexual abuse 14-22
  professionals' perception of 11-12,
  38, 56, 60, 66
  rates 1985-1989 27
sexual injuries 8, 14, 16, 20-22
sexually transmitted diseases 8, 10,
  20-21
siblings 8-10, 14, 24
  see also families
signs of abuse 7-28
sites of injury 13-14, 16
social development, distorted 8, 17

social workers
  confusion about role 31, 75-6
  links with children and parents 2
  models of investigation 9, 14
  need for support 36-8, 59, 66-7
  see also professionals
special needs, abuse of children with
  24-5, 48-50
Speller, Bridie 73-9
spending on children's services,
  Oxfordshire 42-4
staff vetting in day care 47-8
standards in day care 33, 46-8
stereotyping 66-7
Stevenage Family Centre 73-9
suicide 15
support/supervision system for staff
  36-8, 59, 66-7
support/supervision system for
  volunteers 84-5
survival mechanisms 11-12
survivors *see* abused children
switching off *see* dissociation
Sykes, Rob 40-50
symptoms of abuse 7-28
syphilis *see* sexually transmitted
  diseases

T
teachers
  role in child protection 9, 26, 58-70
  support/supervision system 36, 59
  training needs 54-5, 65-7
  see also early years services;
    education; professionals
therapy
  abused children 25-6
  families 36, 73-6
  see also counselling; psychologists
thrive, failure to 8, 22-3
torture 20-22
training
  assertiveness 37
  in child protection 38, 48, 53-7
  early years workers 65-7
  funding 44, 46-7, 54, 86